Kids Killing Kids

Linda Mintle, Ph.D.

with

Larry Keefauver, D.Min.

KIDS KILLING KIDS by Linda Mintle
Published by Creation House
Strang Communications Company
600 Rinehart Road
Lake Mary, Florida 32746
www.creationhouse.com
www.charismalife.com

Library of Congress Catalog Card Number: 99-74172
International Standard Book Number: 0-88419-669-0

In order to protect the privacy of Dr. Mintle's clients,
case stories recorded in this book are composite illustrations
from the histories of several individuals.

9012345 BBG 87654321
Printed in the United States of America

Praise be to the God and Father of our Lord Jesus Christ, the Father of compassion and the God of all comfort, who comforts us in all our troubles, so that we can comfort those in any trouble with the comfort we ourselves have received from God.
—2 CORINTHIANS 1:3–4, NIV

We are praying for the families who lost loved ones in such a sudden and incomprehensible way. May God console your hurting hearts and comfort you in these days of mourning.

CASSIE BERNALL	STEVEN ROBERT CURNOW
COREY DEPOOTER	KELLY FLEMING
MATTHEW KECHTER	DANIEL MAUSER
DANIEL ROHRBOUGH	WILLIAM DAVID SANDERS
RACHEL SCOTT	ISAIAH SHOELS
JOHN TOMLIN	LAUREN TOWNSEND
KYLE VELASQUEZ	

Acknowledgments

I wish to express my gratitude . . .

To God, who provides us with all we need to accomplish His purposes.

To my husband, Norm, for undergirding me with his time and talent. Thank you for being such a good father to our son and daughter.

To my mom and dad for once again sacrificing their time to help me with the children. You have always been there, lending a helping hand and generously giving of yourselves.

To my friend Bunny Mirrilees, for helping me in the small but meaningful ways.

To all my prayer partners.

To the other members of the ERTW for the long days and nights of nonstop writing. Your assistance was invaluable. You made it happen.

To Dave Welday, Rick Nash and all the wonderful people at Creation House, who made this dream a reality.

Table of Contents

The Shepherd's Psalm

The LORD is my shepherd;
    I shall not want.
He maketh me to lie down in
    green pastures:
he leadeth me beside the still
    waters.
He restoreth my soul:
he leadeth me in the paths of
    righteousness
for his name's sake.

Yea, though I walk through the
    valley of the shadow of death,
I will fear no evil:
for thou art with me;
thy rod and thy staff they
    comfort me.
Thou preparest a table before me
    in the presence of mine enemies:
thou anointest my head with oil;
my cup runneth over.
Surely goodness and mercy shall
    follow me
all the days of my life:
and I will dwell in the house
    of the LORD
for ever.

—PSALM 23, KJV

What I saw was death and destruction, ugliness and evil, pain and sorrow. But in my mind I could also visualize what it was the kids were doing prior to this tragic event: homework, chatting about weekend events, flirting. And what kids do. It made me want to hug each one of them as they lay there.

—Alex Woods, Sr.,
Denver bomb squad officer
as he first viewed the carnage in the
Columbine High School library

Preface

In stunned horror, I watched the reports about the Columbine High School students. As the tragedy unfolded, I knew that millions of parents like me would first grieve for the loss of these children and then wonder:

- Could this happen in our school?

- What would I do, and how would I cope if it were my son or daughter?

- What about the shooters—what went wrong?

- Could what went wrong with them go wrong in my kids?

- Am I missing signs of trouble in my own children?

Impossible, I thought. *It couldn't happen here.* But sadly, the parents in Littleton, Colorado, as well as in Kentucky, Oregon and Arkansas, all believed it couldn't happen there, and it did. Why?

No book can give all the answers, nor should it try. But there are *some* answers, and more importantly, there are some things we can believe and ways we can respond.

We love our teens deeply; they are wonderful gifts from God. We want to protect and guide them. And we desperately desire to keep them and others from being enveloped by the lonely, alienated web of estrangement and private pain that plummeted not only the shooters but our culture into grief.

It's true that high school shootings are rare, but that they exist at all is a wake-up call for parents, teachers, administrators, counselors, church leaders, politicians and law enforcement officials. We cannot be silent. We must face and talk about:

- Lost boys and private pain.

- Family pain that contributes to kids killing kids.

- Media pain that torments, addicts and overdoses our kids with violence through the impact of TV, films, music and games.

- The pain of grief and anxiety as we respond to these tragedies.

- The spiritual pain of trying to understand God's love and comfort in the midst of suffering.

Above all else, we must fear no evil.

Are we helpless or hopeless? This book proclaims a resounding *No!* Because for us as Christians the specter of death is not the final word. Christ's resurrection has forever shattered death's power. And the God who loves us goes with us through every storm, through every sudden, unexplained tragedy in life.

You need not fear what you will learn in this book about violence in our schools, among our teens, in our families and permeating the media. These facts are not meant to incite fear, but they are intended to wake us up. As Christians, we cannot ignore what happens in our schools or culture with kids. So this book brings us face to face with the facts and also offers practical tools to use in responding to the pain. In this book you will:

- Uncover the background behind the individual pain that surfaced at these school shootings.

- Learn about lost boys, about private pain and how to keep that pain from destroying your kids and family.

- Become informed about the "risk factors" and "warning signs" of the influence of violence on your teens.

- Unmask the culture of violence that insidiously lures kids into the traps of hate, crime, rage and destructive behavior.

- Understand how to handle grief in the aftermath of tragedy.

- Be equipped with practical steps to take for creating a healthy emotional and spiritual atmosphere for your teen.

- Discover biblical truths about what God is doing in the midst of tragedy and how His good overcomes evil in the world.

Violence has mounted an attack on our culture. How dangerous is this attack? Lt. Col. David Grossman, creator of "Killology," a study of the process of killing, comments:

> Violence is the single most toxic substance that anyone can ever take into their minds.[1]

This book is a siren announcing that God has given us the wisdom and the power to reach out to alienated teens with caring, understanding and the good news of God's love for them in Christ. Instead of withdrawing or condemning we can become light in darkness, salt in the world and agents for God's change in our schools and culture.

Don't read this book if you want to keep your kid at arm's length.

Don't read this book if you want Littleton to happen again and again.

Don't read this book if you believe that cultural evil is winning the war for our kids' minds and souls.

But if you are ready for hope, power, spiritual warfare and taking back our families and schools through the power of God's Spirit . . . then read on.

Fear no evil. Kids killing kids doesn't have to define our decade. Instead, a new generation inspired by the faithful witness of the eight student Christians martyred at Columbine High School defines who we are. It is a generation exemplified by martyr Cassie Bernall's faith in God and her courageous confession of belief in the face of death.

We, too, are followers of Jesus—overcomers of the night. Cassie's bracelet asked the same question that we now ask and, in part, answer: "What would Jesus do?"

—*Linda Mintle*

Part One:
The Problem

The joys of parents are secret,
and so are their griefs and fears.

—Francis Bacon

"I thought we lived in Pleasantville," said Josiah Pina, a senior at Columbine High School. *"I could see it happening in other places, but not here. Nothing ever happened here."*[1]

I used to worry about safety at my school. But after the Jonesboro shootings, I started to think about it more. Jonesboro is just across the state from here. I just started to think, if it can happen there, it can happen here. This year we had two bomb threats. It was a hoax this time, but it makes me think that next time it may not be.

—Thomas James, age 17
Senior at Northside High School,
Ft. Smith, Arkansas

It Couldn't Happen Here

We know about *urban* violence. We're all too familiar with the nightly news scenes—inner-city neighborhoods besieged by daily shootings, drug dealers hustling small children, gangs raping and murdering, seemingly at will. Urban violence, although horrible in its own right, is often seen as a by-product of the cramped, stressful conditions of city living.

It was only a decade ago that our perception of youth violence was that it happened among poor, inner-city black kids high on crack or other street drugs. As the reports of daily violence resounded from the TVs in our family room we'd take a glance and see kids killing kids. We stared for a moment and mumbled a passing "How sad," and then we went on with our lives. It didn't register: kids killing kids.

We were probably unaware that each year approximately forty teenagers are murdered every week, most of them by guns. If you do the math, that's roughly one hundred fifty Littletons a year.[2] But because these deaths aren't high profile, or because they happen one by one, we tend to ignore the growing violence all around us.

What we haven't prepared ourselves for is the violence taking place in small-town America, with kids killing kids at school.

These kids aren't from the streets. Sometimes they're the kids next door.

Violence ... Comes Home?

It's hard to think about violence coming home. After all, I offer this book to you as a fellow parent who seeks God's comfort in the face of some scary news. My hope is that through these pages you'll gain a confident, courageous spirit and a stronger faith. Yet, as we walk this journey together, and with everyone who cares for teenagers, we simply cannot ignore the ugly signs of a deadly impulse creeping into our society, even in suburbia. Consider:

> *Barry Loukaitis* was a fourteen-year-old honors student when he walked into his algebra class on February 2, 1996, and shot his teacher in the back, two students in the chest. Barry was familiar with guns; his dad had taught him how to shoot. He watched movies like *Natural Born Killers* and even bragged that it would be "pretty cool" to go on a killing spree like the one in the movie. Court records indicate that Barry watched one of the dying

boys choke on his own blood and said, "This sure beats algebra, doesn't it!"

Luke Woodham was heartbroken over the breakup with his girlfriend, Christy. According to reports, his nineteen-year-old buddy, who mentored and tormented him with occult practices, told him to kill his mother to "get revenge on Christy and cause a reign of terror." On the fateful morning of October 1, 1997, he murdered his dog and mother, then drove to school and opened fire on his girlfriend and other schoolmates. In the end, Luke's girlfriend and three students lay dead, with seven others wounded. Luke also mentioned that he'd planned to shoot the mayor's son for the "shock value."

Michael Carneal, the fourteen-year-old son of a lawyer, was patient in his approach. He waited in the lobby of his West Paducah, Kentucky, high school, watching a group of fellow students as they gathered in a hallway prayer circle. When the teens finished praying, Michael drew a pistol and fired— three dead and five wounded. He only stopped shooting after the head of the prayer group talked Carneal into putting down the gun.

Sadly, the list could go on: Kip Kinkel, age fifteen, of Springfield, Oregon, shoots twenty-four students (killing two) in the school cafeteria after first murdering his parents at home.

A young teen in Edinboro, Pennsylvania, shoots and kills his science teacher at a graduation dance.

An eleven-year-old and thirteen-year-old in Jonesboro, Arkansas, set off the school fire alarm and open fire on students from a nearby field, killing four girls, a teacher and wounding ten others.

A school is still one of the safest places your child can be.

A sixteen-year-old in Bethel, Alaska, opens fire with a shotgun in a common area of his high school, killing the principal and another student, wounding two others.

And in Fayetteville, Tennessee, an eighteen-year-old honor student opens fire in the school parking lot, killing a classmate who dated his ex-girlfriend.

How do we respond to such reports? The natural reaction is to shrink back in mind-numbing shock and total disbelief. In Littleton, Colorado, as news of the shootings spread through the community, police led Dylan Klebold's parents to a small plot of grass in the family's yard. The Klebolds couldn't believe their son was involved in the mayhem. Dylan's father, Tom, kept repeating, "This isn't happening. This is absurd. There's nothing you [the police] are going to find. Go ahead and look. I don't care. Dylan's not violent."[3]

Recently I heard a teacher comment on the *Oprah Winfrey Show* that if she'd been asked twenty-four hours prior to the shooting at her school, she would have said that hers was one of the safest campuses in America. But it wasn't a safe school on the day the killing began.

How Safe Are Our Schools?

Parents, I want to be very clear: A school is still one of the safest places your child can be. Nevertheless, the shocking increase in school violence has been sounding an alarm for us as parents, teachers and politicians. It's clear we must take notice. Again: The good news is that less than 1 percent of homicides involving school-age children occur in or around schools. The bad news is that even one murder of a child is too many.

So let's delve a little deeper into the facts involved, as painful as they may be. According to statistics, white children are less at risk for homicide than black; suburban children less than urban; wealthy less than poor; and kids are less at risk at school than *anywhere* else.

But since 1992 the annual death toll from school shootings has more than doubled. In 1997, 8 percent of high school students said they had carried a gun to school in the preceding month. That was down 12 percent from 1993.[4] Still, more than 6,000 American students were kicked out of school in the 1996–97 school year for packing weapons.[5] And nearly one million U.S. students took guns to school in 1998.[6] Here are a few more facts:

- In 1993, Americans were more likely to be killed by a stranger than by a family member or friend.

KIDS KILLING KIDS

- Murder arrests among young people under eighteen increased by 128.1 percent from 1983 to 1992.

- Nearly a million teenagers are victims of violent crime each year.

- Ten percent of all public schools experienced one or more serious violent crimes in the 1996–97 school year.

- Seventy-seven percent of high schools reported one or more violent incidents.

- Seventy-eight percent of schools have some form of violence prevention program.

- Forty-three violent deaths occurred in schools last year. Thirty-five were by shooting.

- Seventy-three percent of schools have security officers, and 33 percent of those officers are armed.[7]

Schools are no longer totally protected and secure. The possibility of violence does exist.

We can't run from violence nor deny the reality that kids are killing kids in the suburbs. Nevertheless, many Americans have moved to the suburbs to be safe. They seek neighbors who share their values. They hope to put their kids in good and safe schools. They're looking for teachers who care and parents who get involved. And many families have found good places to live. Yet, in the suburbs, we have falsely believed that we can create a completely controlled, secure environment. We've succumbed to the illusion that green playgrounds, spacious parks and pleasant community gathering places are totally detached from the urban problems of too little green space, too many gangs and too much violence.

Recently my husband and I had to decide where to live when we moved to the Chicago area. We chose a safe suburb, telling people we had moved to a *Truman Story* community in which neighbors trust and protect one another. Our decision about where to live was based primarily on the proximity of the schools, because we have two children. The public school district we chose is rated highly in our state, but still we decided to put our children in a private school—looking for even more moral and physical security. Even so, in view of the recent school violence, we must grapple with the reality that no place is thoroughly safe. We still live in a violent, hostile world.

One expert in urban violence, Nicky Cruz, observed back in 1995:

> The middle- and upper-class suburbs were content to let those in the inner city destroy themselves. When I first started warning America about the inner-city powder keg, no one projected that the ghettos' problems were going to become everyone's problems, including the suburbs'.[8]

Then in 1998, in an interview about the outbreak of

suburban violence with Pat Robertson on *The 700 Club*, Nicky passionately predicted, "If something doesn't stop this violence, they will kill us all." Maybe we've ignored his warning for too long and have been in a state of denial, believing we can escape the effects of violence in our society. I do often wonder whether we aren't a nation in spiritual slumber with a culture that has not truly taken care of its young. Can these school shootings be a wake-up call to us?

Will Fear Win Out?

Now that we are more acutely aware of the possibility of school violence, what can we do to cope with it and make sure that fear does not win the day? First, we can keep in mind that the chances of violence happening at school are still low. Next, we need to be prepared, knowing that the possibility exists for the reasons laid out in this book. So the challenge is: *How do we confront the realities of school violence while not allowing fear to take over?*

Every day, since we face the reality of a violent world, we continually have to work on not letting fear overtake us. For example, we know that teens are killed in car accidents, face drug and alcohol pressures, are sexually promiscuous at younger ages and can die from diseases such as AIDS. We know that teens feel immortal and take risks that are often unsafe. At age seventeen, I remember hitch hiking. I knew it was unsafe, but thought nothing bad could happen to me. This was naive, but such are the thoughts of a teenager.

Teens are an at-risk group by virtue of their developmental stage. You know this, and that's why parenting a teenager is stressful. So parents of teenagers constantly face uncertainty and feelings of helplessness. We send our kids out and pray that God will protect them and help them make good choices.

What is new about school violence is that it adds another dimension to feeling unsafe and helpless to all of our lives. Put school violence on top of the list of already serious concerns about teenagers, and we feel overwhelmed.

We need to understand what contributes to this violence so that we can try to prevent it and respond appropriately.

We don't need another issue of safety to think about. For some people, coping with this additional element puts them over the edge.

Adults have safety needs as well, of course. In order for us to function in other areas of our lives, we need a sense of safety. We want to have the peace of mind that sending our children to school each day will not result in harm. And our need to have a safe environment, in some measure, depends on the cooperation of other people. Thus, a warm supportive environment at home and school is essential.

Parents Coping With Fear

The challenge, then, is to create a relatively safe environment in which kids feel protected and secure. The task is enormous but not impossible. Yet we also need to find ways to cope with our own fear and anxiety as adults. Consider these two suggestions

1. *Recognize that you will feel anxious.* School violence is such an intense stressor because the lives of our children are at stake. As the parent, you seek a way to make sense of all this yourself. When you know how to deal with fear and anxiety, you can communicate a measure of reassurance to your child.

2. *Ask yourself how you think about school violence.* Is it totally unpredictable? Are there warning signs? Do you feel a sense of hopelessness and fear? Is there anything you can do as a parent to protect your child? How do you see God involved in child protection? These kinds of questions will help clarify your thoughts about school violence.

   School violence is one sign of the times warned about in the Bible. We live in a world in which evil abounds and the consequences of that evil affect us whether we are Christians or not. We can't always prevent bad things from happening, so we must be prepared spiritually for whatever comes.

   This doesn't leave us powerless or fatalistic, however. While we must confront reality head-on, we do have ways to fight evil and take a stand. We can take specific and direct actions to stop violence and the evil forces around us. That's what this book is all about.

In general, Christians must pray and seek God for His intervention. We must be proactive, praying for the protection of our children and asking God to give us wisdom. Wisdom is needed in so many areas. It is time to stop allowing others who are not led by the Spirit to direct our paths. Get on your knees and seriously ask God to direct you and give you wisdom for raising your teens. You may have ideas that inspire schools and give hope.

3. *Recognize the battle is not just against flesh and blood.* The war is also waged against "principalities and powers." God has told us that we have the authority to overcome evil in His name. Are we apathetic on this end, or are we taking this power seriously? Are we waging the war in the spiritual realm? Unite with churches, youth groups and other organizations that feel this burden and intercede and take authority over darkness.

Also, you fill yourself with the promises of God in order to overcome fear and anxiety. His Word calls us to be anxious about nothing. It doesn't say, "except for when it comes to school violence." So apply the command to all things. Rebuke fear from your mind, because of the promises you have from God (see Chapter 6 on faith perspective). By doing this you are not denying the reality of circumstances or the world; rather, you are denying the grip of fear to take hold.

Too many of us walk around confessing the negative and defeated side of life. We are victorious in Christ's name and need to live in victory. This means overcoming the enemy of our minds, who says, "You are never safe. You can never trust God. He's a liar and doesn't protect you." Take hold of these thoughts, and rebuke them in the name of Jesus. We serve the God of the impossible. All things are possible with God.

4. *Defeat fear by acting in unfearful ways.* We need to pay attention to signs of trouble around us and not be afraid to act on our intuitions. Are you afraid to report kids for fear that the kid will retaliate or that his parents will become angry? Too many of us are apathetic and uninvolved with our own children to know what they are doing. We have to act with authority. There is a wealth of information on what you can do in this book.

We may also need to become more politically active when it comes to issues such as school prayer and juvenile justice. Ask God to show you if you are to be a part of standing for righteousness in the culture at large.

5. *Reach out in relationship.* Fear is defeated through relationship, first through an intimate relation-

ship with our Father and Creator, and next through intimacy with teens. Research clearly shows that teens who are emotionally connected with a meaningful adult are less likely to act out. Get connected. Mentor a child and care about those who are lost.

We can reach out to kids emotionally and physically, and support financial programs that help them or that structure their time in meaningful and spiritual ways. People need to be in community and help take care of kids who are struggling. We are all so busy and have become so self centered that we don't see the needs around us.

Teens Coping With Fear

Are your teens confident that adults are doing all they can to insure their safety? Teens should not be responsible for determining who among them is stable or unstable. They do need to report irregularities, suspicions and behavior changes that they see. But the major responsibility to act should fall on school administrators, teachers, counselors and parents.

We all know that safety is a basic human need. Kids need to feel protected, secure, have structure and be relatively free from chaos in order to learn. They want to be in an environment that reinforces their security and reflects a consistent and structured approach to any problem. When the basic need of safety is thwarted, fear and anxiety result.

Unfortunately, recent violence has made teens uneasy, anxious and fearful about going to school. We have to help our kids deal with the reality of violence but not get caught up in the fear ourselves.

Get connected. Mentor a child and care about those who are lost.

Teens worry a lot about being a rat—someone who tells on another kid. They also have bought the cultural message that kids in trouble are not their immediate problem. Someone else will deal with it. As mentioned above, teens should be encouraged to report all fears, suspicions and worries to a caring adult. We then have a responsibility to follow up on those concerns and report back to the teen on steps taken. Feedback on steps taken reduces fear.

While I was writing this book, two things happened. First, a few weeks after Littleton, a twelve-year old child was found carrying a loaded gun in a suburban elementary school in the Chicago area. According to news reports, he was mad at two other boys and decided to take a loaded gun to school to scare them. A teacher noticed the gun under his clothes, and the student was disarmed.

Disaster averted.

But the parents interviewed on the news were clearly distraught and rethinking their options about sending their children back to school. The kids were terrified by these incidents and fearful as well. Many refused to go to school. This type of incident is repeated in several other places. Copy cat crimes are reported and we are more aware of threats.

One thing we can do is tell kids what measures have been reviewed, instituted or changed to deal with these incidents. Teens should know what consequences followed these types of behavior. Don't leave them hanging with just the facts of the incident. Report the follow up.

Another thing we can do is answer kids' questions—constantly. When they are close to it, teens talk frantically about all the possibilities of violence. Now that teens are aware of school violence, they need to be informed and directed in positive ways. Hold special forums to discuss the problems. Help them brainstorm ways to confront difficult kids. Help them with conflict resolution. Role-play situations in which violence may occur and anticipate what to do.

Information is helpful because it lessens the feeling of being out of control and helps teens have a more realistic view of what really happened. Without information, teens are more likely to make things up which could be exaggerated or wrong.

They also become frightened by rumors. It helps them to think before a situation occurs and not just to respond to a crisis. There will be many programs developed after these shootings to help kids do these things. As more information surfaces about each act of violence in schools we are able to see signs and patterns that emerge. For example we know there were warning signs in each shooting. Knowing that the boys who shot gave signals should allay some fears. The more we know, the better we can prepare and take threats seriously.

Being a teenager has its own stress apart from school violence. Unlike kids in previous generations, today's teens are often faced with issues far before they are developmentally ready to deal with them. For example, I have an increasing number of thirteen and fourteen year olds talking about decisions to sleep with their boyfriends/girlfriends, whether they should engage in pornographic acts and how they should handle drugs and alcohol. They have been exposed to adult issues far before their readiness to handle them. What results is teens with knowledge and experience who lack the coping abilities and emotional development to respond appropriately. Therefore, we have to work with teens on what is appropriate for them at given their developmental ages.

We need to set standards of behavior and encourage programs that delay the introduction of adult themes into their lives. I also think we need to be more careful about exposure to most adult issues. I know we can't always control what our teens see and hear, but many times we can. For example, watch your conversations and make them appropriate to the level of the teen, turn off violent programs and monitor the Internet. (More suggestions will come in later chapters.)

How to Evaluate the Safety of Schools . . .

We can ask some basic questions that will likely help improve school safety and identify teens at risk. This is by no means a comprehensive list, but it will help you begin a dialogue with schools.

- Do school administrators have in place school district policies that are well developed, defined and defensible legally? Policies should include ways to deal with threats, damaging property, hitting, bullying and more.

- Are school policies explicit and do they clearly define the infractions for breaking the rules? Are you as a parent or teen aware of these policies?

- Do officials have a plan to deal specifically with threats? When does the school notify parents about a problem student? What does the school define as problem behaviors needing parental involvement? What is the expectation for the school and for parents regarding action and follow up?

- Does the school have a violence prevention plan and has it been communicated to parents and students? Does the school have a way for teens to report concerns and other kids, e.g., an Anonymous tip line?

- Does the school have a zero tolerance policy toward violence—both verbal and behavioral? Does the administration back up teachers who worry about specific kids? How does that happen?

- How do school psychologists and guidance counselors get alerted about at-risk kids? Is there a child study team? Are there enough psychologists and counselors to handle the demand?

- How well does the school utilize community resources and network with at-risk programs and services?

- Are their guidelines for Internet use specially regarding chat rooms and e-mail correspondence?

- Is there a dress code? Are teens allowed to wear shirts with violent messages such as "Serial Killer" on them?

- Is there a conflict resolution program or social skills training? Is there a place where alternatives to violence are discussed? What is being done to counteract the violent messages teens are given by the culture? How are cliques and gangs handled by the school? Does the school have a unified discipline plan?

- Does the school offer friendship and ways for a teen to join programs based on interests? This relates to special interests like math clubs, book clubs, band and others. It also raises the question of funding for extracurricular activities in communities in which kids spend a lot of time unsupervised after school.

- Does the school use metal detectors, random searches or have security cameras or people on watch? Does it use volunteer parents and teacher aides to monitor the halls? You need to know what the school has in place.

- What is the student-teacher ratio? The more teachers are overwhelmed by class numbers, the less they can know each teen. Teens become a number not a person when ratio of student to teacher is high.

- Does anyone track records of kids with problems? Are those kids receiving help or have they fallen through the cracks?

- How well do all school personnel know the warning signs of kids at risk?

Will It Happen Again?

I know the violence we've witnessed won't go away simply because we choose to turn our backs to it. We need to understand what contributes to this violence so we can try to prevent it and respond appropriately. Obviously, something more than normal adolescent development is involved when a kid walks into his school and fires away. I think of a statement I came across somewhere on the Internet a few days ago attributed to Andrew Molchan, director of the National Association of Federally Licensed Gun Dealers:

> Somebody doesn't decide to walk into a school and murder several people because of lack of a gun lock or something. It's a horrible, profound, moral issue.

He's right, isn't he? As much as we may abhor the amount and availability of guns in our society, we still recognize that it's *not* normal to shoot people as a way of coping with painful feelings. What, then, influences certain kids to commit such horrific crimes? These are not Sunday school kids having a bad day. Nor are they gangsters or kids from an inner-city ghetto. These are teens that have probably lived next door to people like us, spent the night in homes like ours. They play video games and watch movies with our kids. Can it happen here?

Yet we are not hopeless or totally helpless. We can do something about it as we trust in God's strength and sovereignty. Love, after all, is the greatest power in the universe. Our love for our youth—and God's overwhelming love for them—will ultimately overcome every barrier that keeps us from relating to one another with deep and abiding affection. Until then we persevere, day by day, in hope and faith. Without fear.

> We are pressed on every side by troubles, but we are not crushed and broken. We are perplexed, but we don't give up and quit. We are hunted down, but God never abandons us. We get knocked down, but we get up again and keep going.
>
> —2 CORINTHIANS 4:8–9, NLT

My life and the lives of my children are in Your loving hands, dear Lord. I will fear no evil, for You are with me—always.

Part Two:
The "Why?"

———————— **2** ————————

Although the world is full of suffering,
it is also full of the overcoming of it.

—Helen Keller

When I approach a child,
he inspires in me two sentiments:
tenderness for what he is,
and respect for what he may become.

—Louis Pasteur

Lost Boys and Private Pain

The finest kids in America pass through these halls. The engraved proclamation greets every person who walks under the hallway arch in Littleton's Columbine High School. So what made two of America's finest kids suddenly become killers?

Or was it not so sudden, after all?

Were there any patterns of behavior emerging over the years? Any qualities of personality that started developing in these boys well before the horrible day of violence?

Can We Detect Something Here?

One of the big questions on the minds of all of us is this: How do we detect and understand a kid who might kill other kids?

First, before you read further, I invite you to let this sink in: *The two boys in Littleton were solely to blame for the evil they perpetrated on others.* It was their choice, and theirs alone. The terrible campus massacre was not the parents' fault, the school officials' fault, the community's fault, my fault or your fault. In spite of the outrage reported daily from radio and television regarding how "we are all in some sense to blame," the fact remains: Two young boys committed evil acts. Even if warning signs were available to us, even if we see later how an act might have been prevented, it is wrong to blame innocent folks for the sins of others.

I'm simply trying to say that my heart is broken for the families and communities who have been living through so much grief. Anyone who experiences sudden trauma and death takes on a long-lasting woundedness. It is no time for casting blame. In a way, we are all in shock after the recent tragedies, and we are called to reach out and comfort one another. We can take refuge in the hope of the gospel.

Those boys were in so much pain, too, and our hearts are surely broken for them as well. It's also true that we are wise to begin learning how to watch for dysfunction in our culture and in our young men. We could very well pick up on something that might signal the potential for future tragedy. We do know, for instance, that kids who end up killing tend to have certain characteristics. So let's take a closer look at the bright, full-of-potential but lost boys in Littleton—Eric and Dylan. Both came from two-parent, upper-middle class families and did normal teenage things—they bowled, worked at a pizza parlor, enjoyed scouting and baseball. Nevertheless, in retrospect, warning signs were present.

According to news reports and commentators, the lost boys showed certain signs of trouble. Rejected by their peers and considered the outcasts of the school, they banded together in a subgroup named after one of the most violent groups in the world—the Mafia. They called themselves "The Trench Coat Mafia." Parading in long, black dusters and wearing combat boots, they embraced the Goth aesthetic, idolized Hitler, spoke German, wore swastikas, made racist remarks, hated Jews, Hispanics and African Americans and wore armbands proclaiming "I Hate People."

The Trench Coat Mafia boys appeared to be disconnected (except to each other in their cause), unpopular and ridiculed. These were lost boys who identified aggression and violence as a solution for stopping their pain. The plan was to get revenge (through homicide) and then react to the hopelessness of their own lives (through suicide).

In addition to being a part of the Mafia subgroup, this duo reportedly also:

- Was obsessed with death.

- Professed to despise God.

- Wrote about killing people in school projects.

- Made a mock video of killing student athletes.

- Bragged about blowing up the school and getting new guns.

- Was fascinated with weapons and obsessed with explosives.

- Found information about bomb making on the Internet.

- Obsessively played violent video games.

- Favored violent martial arts movies.

- Talked about violence.

In particular, Eric Harris reportedly:

- Shoved girls and was known as a bully toward girls.

- Maintained a violent Web site.

- Proclaimed two years earlier that he wanted to blow up the high school.

- Talked about "going postal" and shooting someone he was mad at.

- Was rejected by the Marines because he lied about being on Luvox, an antidepressant used to treat an obsessive-compulsive disorder.

- Said he would like to be on the front lines in Serbia and kill a lot of people.

In a psychology class, both boys had written a project about Goth idol Marilyn Manson and serial killer Jeffrey Dahmer. Interestingly enough, on the day of the killings, Dylan's T-shirt was emblazoned with the trademark label "Serial Killer."

Shared Similarities

The Colorado shooters shared certain similarities with previous school shooters.

First, all were teenage Caucasians with above-average intelligence. After Dylan and Eric were arrested for breaking into a commercial van and stealing electronics, Klebold's diversion officer wrote in a report, "Dylan is a bright young man who has a great deal of potential. He is intelligent enough to make any dream a reality, but he needs to understand that hard work is a part of it." Harris's officer wrote, "Eric is a very bright young man who is likely to succeed in life. He is intelligent enough to achieve lofty goals as long as he stays on task and remains motivated."[1] Nonetheless, most shooters have felt inferior or picked on by fellow students. Theirs were the normal adolescent complaints of being too fat, too short, unloved, etc., but their responses were depression and suicidal imaginings. These were kids stressed out with unhappy lives. Their solution? To kill as a way to end their tortured existence.

Second, each of the alleged teen killers had easy access to guns with rapid-fire capacities. We aren't talking one-shot pistols. These were guns capable of firing automatic rounds able to do harm multiple times over. In some cases, par-

> *These were kids stressed out with unhappy lives. Their solution? To kill as a way to end their tortured existence.*

ents taught the teens how to shoot those weapons. Given the fact that many teens have an underdeveloped sense of the finality of death, putting powerful firearms at their disposal is truly unwise. While some teens may be able to handle such a responsibility, these kids could not. Remember Kip Kinkel? According to reports, he loved guns. His obsession with guns was so intense that his parents bought him one "to control and connect with their volatile child." Yet I have to wonder: Why would anyone give a gun to an angry teenager?

Third, these kids wrote and talked about killing people. In one TV interview, two friends of a shooter said they heard him talk about hurting animals and wanting to hurt people. Apparently, they didn't believe him. Even when they do believe, kids don't always report on other kids in trouble. They don't want to "rat" on a friend.

Fourth, our violent culture affected each of these kids. In addition to occult influences over some, most were certainly influenced by violent rap messages, entertainers like Marilyn Manson, movies with killing sprees, violent video games, and TV and Internet violence. Teens are highly susceptible to these powerful images.

How is it possible that such evil lurks in the souls of some of our children? The apostle Paul himself wrote of the tenor of this age, declaring:

> You should also know this, Timothy, that in the last days there will be very difficult times. For people will love only themselves and their money. They will be boastful and proud, *scoffing at God, disobedient to their parents,* and ungrateful. *They will*

> *consider nothing sacred. They will be unloving and unforgiving;* they will slander others and have no self-control; they will be cruel and have no interest in what is good. *They will betray their friends, be reckless, be puffed up with pride, and love pleasure rather than God.*
> —2 TIMOTHY 3:1–4, EMPHASIS ADDED

Yes, we do have a problem with evil. On the other hand, think of all the normal teens walking around in your neighborhood. There is such a thing as an "OK kid." In fact, he or she is probably staring at you across the breakfast table right now. (Go ahead, pass him the corn flakes.) The point is, in order to understand when a particular teenager is potentially violent, we must first define some of the developmental characteristics of all those normal adolescents.

The Normal Kid

The thing to realize is that children are unique in their responses to developmental transitions and life events. Their responses depend on a number of factors that include both biology and environment. Most mental health professionals agree on markers for normative adolescent development and define it in three stages—early, middle and late adolescence. Below is a brief summary of what typically happens in teen development.[2]

Early adolescence (12–14)

This stage involves the struggle to find a sense of identity and the movement toward independence. Teens at this age are better able to express themselves but tend to do so by actions rather than words. They are often moody and occasionally rude. Peer group influences, with an emphasis on close friendships, gain significant importance. Looking for new people to love, these kids pay less attention to their parents, whom they no longer regard as perfect. They can be childish. They worry about being normal. This is the time when they may begin to experiment with various substances.

> *Children are unique in their responses to developmental transitions and life events.*

Middle adolescence (15–17)

Teens now tend to become more self-involved, examining their inner experiences by writing in a diary or by identifying with the lyrics of popular music. They go through periods of sadness as they try to negotiate separation from their parents, often complaining that parents interfere with their move toward independence. Identification with the peer group grows stronger and so do concerns over appearance and making new friends.

These adolescents can delay gratification, think through abstract ideas, express ideas in words and make independent decisions. They're becoming more emotionally stable, able to compromise, developing a full-blown sense of humor. In this stage, self-esteem grows stronger as teens set goals and increase their capacity for sophisticated insight.

Late adolescence (17–19)

At this stage, youth form a firmer identity with the ability to delay gratification and think through complicated ideas. Most develop a concern for others, for the future and for their role in life. Personal dignity and self-esteem are more emphasized, in the context of taking on a better sense of self-regulation.

Overall, adolescence is a time of many physical and emotional changes. As one high school teacher put it: "Recall (if you dare) what it is like to be not quite an adult, not quite independent, and not quite sure of who you are."[3] So in light of all the swirling ups and downs, it's quite normal for teens to be deeply upset when a relationship breaks up or to be angry with a friend. Teens like to be weird and go for shock value. They take extreme steps to be different, and they want their privacy. As noted above, their attention shifts away from family and moves to their peers. They are self-conscious, with an extreme focus on thoughts and feelings. Risk taking without thinking through the consequences is common.

Risk Factors and Warning Signs

The question for most parents, teachers and counselors is this: When does a teen show signs of deviating from normal adolescent development? In other words, when are kids in trouble? Sadly one of the most useful things to emerge from the school shootings is a clear set of warning signs. So what do we look for?

A *risk factor* indicates the possibility that something dangerous can happen, but it doesn't mean it will. A *warning sign* is a behavior that has been connected to violence.

Please understand that not every child who exhibits one or more of these warning signs will become a violent killer. But in each of the violent incidents we've been discussing, one or more of these signs were present. Be alert to these signs. Often friends and teachers have tragically commented that the warning signs were likely present but went unnoticed.

Listed below are some risk factors and warning signs associated with violent behavior among kids.

Risk Factors

- Delinquent acts starting at an early age or a history of violence and aggression

- A family history of criminal violence

- Family problems—divorce, multiple moves, financial stress, abuse, alienation, etc.

- Individual psychiatric history—suicide attempts, depression, anxiety, conduct problems, antisocial behavior, etc.

- Prior arrests and criminal activity

- Having a neurological problem that impairs thinking or feeling

- History of discipline problems at school, home and/or in the community

- Peer conflicts and relationships conflicts, including girl problems
- Unable to manage emotions
- Easy access to guns and information about explosives
- Lack of parental supervision
- Constant exposure to violent pop culture
- Dabbling in the occult

Warning Signs

- Risk taking that included violent acts
- Difficulty with authority figures
- Obsession with violent pop culture—music, videos, TV, movies, Internet and video or fantasy games
- Belonging to a gang or involved in a violent subculture
- Substance abuse
- Use of a weapon
- Lack of friends (peer or adult)
- Purposelessness and hopelessness
- Problems trusting others
- Cruelty to animals
- Lack of empathy for others—little regard for the feelings of others

- View others as objects to be acted on

- Rejected by conventional cliques

- Failure at school and declining grades

- Increased isolation from others

- New gang of friends unknown by parents

- Decrease in school involvement or activities

- Overall sense of rejection and loneliness

- Selfishness

- Fascination with weapons and explosives

- Anger-management problems, rage and jealousy

- Feeling disrespected, bullied and unappreciated

- Talk about hurting others

- Signs of depression—persistent sadness, sleep changes, appetite changes, lack of pleasure in most activities, weight changes, agitation, restlessness, fatigue, feelings of worthlessness, excessive or inappropriate guilt, concentration problems, thoughts and/or attempts at suicide. [4]

Each child is unique, a special creation of God with talents, abilities, personality, preferences, dislikes, potentials, strengths, weaknesses and skills that are his or her own. As parents, we must seek to identify these in each of our children and help them become the persons God intended. [5]

The words above are encouraging to me. They assume that we can, indeed, identify what's happening in our children. We can then use that information to shape and mold them for a healthy life in God's kingdom. One of the things we can particularly watch for in our young boys is this: covered-up emotional pain.

Boys Coping With Pain

What do we teach boys when it comes to handling their emotional pain? Too often we teach them that aggression and anger are the only appropriate responses. After all, they are "little men" who need to learn the lessons of big men. For example, too often they are taught:

- "Crying is for sissies."
- "Don't show your weaknesses."
- "Take it like a man."
- "Hide your feelings."
- "Keep others at a distance."
- "If others hurt you, hurt them back."
- "Don't be a momma's boy."

Early on, many boys learn to repress their emotional pain and turn off their feelings. Behind the calm facades hide hurt, sad and depressed young men unable to find an outlet for those feelings except through anger. Repressed pain then turns into rage. Instead of talking about what they feel, lost boys pound desks, throw objects and hit something or someone. Eventually they lose track of what they feel. Consider the case of John:

It was 10:00 A.M.—time for me to go get John from group home #2 on the pretty grounds of a youth residential facility. It was our therapy time. For one hour on Wednesday, John would try to explain his life to me. He didn't think I could help, but he needed to do something. John was a quiet, shy boy with an infectious smile. He always had a new joke for me and made me promise I would laugh, even if the punch line wasn't funny.

But John was depressed. Even though he tried, he had little to say about life. Unlike most nine-year-olds, John found nothing that interested him. He spent his days reading, isolated from others. John's pain was silent. For the past year, he struggled with feelings of worthlessness. He wished he could just vanish. He hated school because the other kids made fun of him, and no one would sit with him during lunch. The neighborhood kids called him a nerd; nobody played with him.

Last week John was at school. As he went to sit down at his desk, someone pulled his chair away, and he fell to the ground. The kids started to laugh. Embarrassed and ashamed, John ran from the room and started hitting his locker. Then he started hitting his head. He pounded and pounded until he fell to the ground.

Once again, John wanted to vanish.

Moments like these were played over and over in John's short life. Finally, John had a plan. His father had a gun, and once and for all, John would vanish . . .

In contrast to boys like John, girls are typically

encouraged to process feelings, talk to adults and cry. Pain is not a sign of weakness for them but a warning that something is wrong. We give girls permission to be sad, and we take them seriously when they express their hurts. Perhaps this is why none of the shooters have been girls—they are encouraged to verbalize and express their pain directly. When girls feel pain, they tend to turn inward and direct it toward their own bodies (thereby generating such problems as eating disorders, self-mutilation, perfectionism and anxiety). However, boys tend to do the opposite of externalizing their anger in appropriate expression—they internalize it until it explodes. Then it hurts others and eventually themselves.

Danny towered over me at six feet, two inches tall. He was a physically imposing young fourteen-year-old referred for threatening a fellow student and punching a hole in the wall of the cafeteria. Danny wanted me to know how tough he was. After years of being taunted for not wanting to play sports, he'd had enough from his peers. He was angry and wanted to get even.

"I hate those kids. How dare they treat me this way! They ain't seen nothing yet. When I get mad, I get even. No one is going to pick on me anymore."

As we walked through the park, I asked, "Other than at school, does anyone pick on you? Have you been pushed around before?"

Danny looked away and started digging in the dirt. After a few minutes he said, "Maybe. I don't want to talk about it. It's no big deal. I can take care of myself. Look at me. I'm a big guy. They'll all be sorry now."

Slowly Danny began to open up. I finally learned that

Danny had been beaten by his dad most of his life. Years of rage had built within him, but it wasn't his rage I was so interested in at the moment. One time, Danny hit back, and his sister called the police. When they arrived, his mom reported that Danny went wild for no apparent reason. Hurt and betrayed, Danny left the house. The pain was intense. The next day, he hit a student.

Danny could hardly recall these events without his eyes watering. "It's OK to cry with me," I said. I tried to reassure him, but it took time before tears fell and the dam of pain and hurt was gradually released.

"I want my dad to love me. I want him to stop hurting me. I want it all to go away."

What Can We Do?

Let me say it again: We have been shaken by these shootings, but we are not hopeless with our teenagers (like Danny), nor helpless in the face of evil. There are even some very practical steps we can take.

> Rescue the poor and helpless;
>> deliver them from the grasp of evil
>> people.
> But these oppressors know nothing;
>> they are so ignorant!
> And because they are in darkness,
>> the whole world is shaken to the core.
>> —PSALM 82:4–5

Generally speaking, any teen that exhibits the warning signs listed earlier needs to be reported to someone—parents, parents' friends, peers, school personnel, police, youth workers, pastors, counselors or other significant adults. In addition to reporting suspicions, other positive steps can be taken to reduce the possibility of kids killing kids:

Develop one-on-one relationships with teens.

There's no substitute for personal relationships between children and healthy adult role models and mentors. Kids who are connected to others in a healthy way act out less. And, of course, it can be a lot of fun to hang around with a teenager.

One way to develop a relationship is to just provide plenty of space for talking. Take the kid fishing and listen! In the process, you can help a boy learn how to identify and manage his emotions, how to find appropriate ways to express hurt and pain.

There's no substitute for personal relationships between children and healthy adult role models and mentors.

Since most boys need help sharing their feelings directly, make the setting safe and free from interruption. They will engage in dialogue better if you engage in an activity; give them space and let it happen. Don't use shaming language. Sometimes it helps to share your own feelings and experiences.

One other thing: Be sure to ask open-ended questions

. . . and let silence be OK. Then simply reflect back to them the feelings they share. For example: "Oh, so you've been feeling sad lately." Or: "I guess that must have hurt pretty bad." Or: "Seems like you've been angry, huh?"

Especially try to reach out to and talk with isolated kids. Many teens feel they're just a number in the sea of students that pass them by daily. An adult who takes notice, with genuine friendliness, can be a life saver.

Refer depressed kids for help.

Various studies have revealed that depression among children has increased 1000 percent since the 1950s. Teen suicide has increased 300 percent since the 1960s.[6] Look for signs of gloom, loss of interest in activities, low self-esteem, irritability, school underachievement, social withdrawal, appetite changes, sleep difficulty, concentration problems and excessive tiredness. Teens who show signs of depression should be evaluated by a mental health professional or trained helping professional: The family should also become involved.

Deal with family problems.

We know that unhappy homes are related to juvenile delinquency and mental illness. For example, in the case of Barry Loukaitis, his mother told him a few weeks before the shooting that her marriage was in trouble and that she was suicidal. There may also be substance abuse in the family, with the teen involved. Get treatment for the young person. In many cases drugs and alcohol are involved in their violent behavior.

Identify bullies—the earlier the better.

Catch them at an early age. Kids who are mercilessly teased and harassed may later bully others and take revenge. The National School Safety Center calls bullying "the most enduring and underrated problem in American schools." Kids identified as bullies at age eight are three times as likely as other youth to break the law by age thirty.[7]

Take it seriously when someone talks of hurting animals or people.

Report this to an adult or the authorities. Encourage teens to report others if this type of talk is heard. They may save lives.

Bring back supervised, extracurricular activities.

Whether at school, home, church or community settings, teens need to stay active. Kids have too much unsupervised, discretionary time. The average adolescent spends 3.5 hours alone daily. Adolescents spend much less time today with their parents than they did in the 1960s.[8]

Don't ignore peer conflicts.

Equip children with appropriate social and conflict-resolution skills. For example, we know there was an ongoing rivalry between the athletes and the Trench Coat Mafia gang at Columbine High School but no resolution to the conflict.

Years ago, as a teacher consultant for Chicago area schools, I did social skills training with teens. I asked the teens to write some brief descriptions of difficult social situations they faced. Then we role-played various ways to handle these situations constructively. I especially focused on the difficulty of making the right choice in the face of strong peer pressure. We discussed the consequences of choosing violent strategies and revenge.

A key point here is that we can teach kids to respect others. They need to understand the impact of teasing, making fun of others or discriminating against those who are different from them.

Do report any violent acts to authorities and counselors. Refer kids who exhibit difficulty relating to authority figures. Refer kids who cannot trust people and lack empathy for others. These symptoms are serious signs are of interpersonal disturbances.

Address gang and subgroup formation.

When kids form a gang of any type, adults need to know the purpose of the gang, whom the members admire and what behaviors they are encouraging. Destructive gangs need to be stopped. Obviously school officials at Columbine High School were unaware of the dynamics of the Trench Coat Mafia, or they would not have allowed them to have a picture in the school yearbook.

Restrict access to guns.

Teens often buy guns near their home towns. It is alarmingly easy to get lethal weapons, and kids have been desensitized by movies and other media as to the actual damage and finality guns cause. Unfortunately, guns are glamorized by the media. They are not for play, and the responsibility of having a gun is immense. Even though many of the accused assailants were properly trained in gun use, this didn't prevent the misuse of a firearm. Knowledge and will are separate things.

Continue to monitor and mentor offender teens.

Kids who have completed diversion or corrective programs for juvenile offenses still need to be watched Parents, teachers and counselors can do this monitoring. Completing a program of remedial steps does not mean the problem has gone away. Keep checking behavior. Get reports. Talk to the teens directly. Talk with other kids about what they are doing and ask the adults who are involved in their lives—the coaches, teachers, youth workers, relatives and neighbors.

Finally, introduce kids to the plan of salvation at an early age.

While no one ever wants to think about losing a child to violence, we have a responsibility to prepare children spiritually for whatever may come.

> For if you confess with your mouth that Jesus is
> Lord and believe in your heart that God raised
> him from the dead, you will be saved. For it is by
> believing in your heart that you are made right
> with God, and it is by confessing with your
> mouth that you are saved.
>   —ROMANS 10:9–10

Many people today are asking where the heroes have
gone for this generation. And it's so true that our young
people, perhaps especially our teenage boys, need heros
and mentors to look up to. Even a secular philosopher
said it:

> The central difficulty in becoming a man
> nowadays is that a boy sees so little of his father
> or other men. A man's work is now separated
> from his home. There are no men around for
> boys to model themselves after. Boys are
> almost exclusively brought up by their
> mothers and taught by women teachers.[9]

Boys certainly need their mothers! But they need good
mentoring men as well. Let me tell you about Bob, a
young man raised by an alcoholic dad. One of the earliest
lessons Bob learned was how to numb himself to emotional pain. His dad did it every day. As a boy, Bob hated
his dad's drinking. Nightly, his dad would begin his slow
descent into an inebriated state while Bob spent most of
his evenings alone or keeping his mother company.

When Bob had a son, he vowed not to drink, but he
found other ways to numb his pain. He first became a

workaholic. But then, as work stress became intense, Bob did begin to drink. Concerned that he "would become his father," he sought help and went to AA meetings.

Bob had to face many painful memories of his childhood and had to learn new ways to cope with that pain. But through the help of God, his family and the church, he was able to do it. He remains sober today.

Bob's son needed him dry, of course. But sobriety wasn't enough. This young boy needed a father who could teach him how to cope with emotional pain. Today, Bob's son is grateful. He now knows what to do when he gets upset, because his dad taught him. Sitting with his son, Bob leans over

The ultimate hero, the healthiest role model of masculinity for the Bobs of this world—and for any man—is Jesus Christ.

and gives me a wink, "I'm so glad I'm sober and can face the world, but the greatest joy is that my son called me his hero. It doesn't get any better than that."

The ultimate hero, the healthiest role model of masculinity for the Bobs of this world—and for any man—is Jesus Christ. Jesus was a man acquainted with pain and grief; He was scorned and tormented, yet nonviolent. (See Isaiah 53.) Jesus showed compassion, caring and tremendous empathy for others in all kinds of circumstances.

And Jesus loves our young people. He loves our boys, the ones who live with us and the ones down the street. Even the ones who suffer deep pain, daily depression or dark impulses to hurt others.

They all need to be taught how to be like Jesus.

> Love your enemies, bless those who curse you, do good to those who hate you and pray for those who spitefully use you and persecute you.
> —MATTHEW 5:44, NKJV

Grant me the grace and courage to reach out, Jesus, just as You always did—to talk to the hurting young man who seems isolated or afraid, to the one who walks by my house every day, the one who's looking my way just now.

In terms of prevention, the single most important, consistent protective factor for youth, across the spectrum of risk behaviors, is parents.

—The Institute for Youth Development

Are we vigilant enough? Most teenagers exist in a state of near constant mortification at the prospect of supervision by their parents. But surely a parent can risk his child's embarrassment, and his own discomfort, to get in his or her face a little bit. Surely we can manage to love them a little louder. To find the time to read their school papers, listen to their music, watch what they watch and get to know their friends. [1]

Relational Pain:
From the Roots Up

I recall the marvelous words of Barbara Bush when she spoke of the importance of the family. "Your success as a family, our success as a society, depends not on what happens at the White House, but on what happens inside your house."[2] The simple point is this: *The behavior of our children is learned behavior.*

Learned mostly at home. Violent behavior, too.

How Barry Learned It

Barry never understood why his father hit him so often. He figured he must be a really bad kid for his dad to get so violent with him. The problem was, Barry never saw it coming. His dad's behavior was unpredictable, so Barry mostly stayed out of his way.

Yet Barry and his dad spent some time together. They loved watching baseball, even though their team lost all the time. When the players made an error, his dad's temper would soar. He'd scream and yell until he was red in the face. When Barry was little, he used to wonder if dad's face was going to explode.

Barry was referred to me for behavior problems with other kids. Like his dad, Barry had a temper. When he didn't get his way, he became physical with boys his age. I asked Barry to tell me how his mom and dad behaved when they didn't get their way. His answer: "Mom goes into the bedroom and closes the door. I don't know what she does in there. Dad yells, throws things and hits me. I guess I do something to make him mad. Most of the time I don't know what it is."

So Barry's mom and dad were asked to join us in therapy. And what I learned is typical of many families who come to see me. Barry's dad, Jim, was hit when he was a child. Jim's dad, an Army officer, wouldn't tolerate mistakes. Jim had to do things exactly as his dad demanded. When he messed up, he was slapped across the face. Much of the time, Jim didn't know what he had done wrong.

Jim was acting as his father taught him. Was his father responsible for Jim's hitting? No. But Jim learned how to deal with his frustration from his father.

He watched, and later he did the same.

Naturally, any child's learning occurs in a number of ways. He or she picks up knowledge and insight from family members, people in the community, peers, the media, cultural icons, the Internet. However, the earliest roots of learning violence can be traced to the family system. Children who aren't taught internal controls (responsibility, morality, spirituality) are more at risk for acting out. Other risk factors include poor monitoring, inconsistent supervision and discipline, abuse in the home and an atmosphere that supports violence.

Relational Pain: From the Roots Up

In this chapter, let's briefly explore some of the psychological factors that affect relational pain in the family, one of the key contributors to a potentially violent child. After we look at the roots of relational pain, I'll suggest some practical ways to handle the hurt.

The Roots of Family Pain

Adolescence is a time of chronic stress and turbulent change—both of which test the limits of a family's ability to cope. In turn, certain responses within the family dynamics either help or hurt a kid's ability to handle stress. My intent here is not to blame or heap guilt on parents. But as a family therapist of twenty years, I have to say that most disturbed kids don't come from families free of dysfunction. On the surface, things may look calm, but underneath a storm can be brewing. I realize that we are all flawed as parents, of course; we do the best we can. And all of us need divine grace and instruction. In that spirit I offer these ten variables to consider when evaluating the roots of pain in your own family:

Variable #1: What are your family stress levels?

Make every effort to reduce the stress in your family. Manage stress; don't let it manage you. For example, when marital problems hit, resolve them privately with your spouse. In fact, it's always best not to overburden children with adult concerns of any kind—financial worries, job problems, neighborhood conflicts. We underestimate the extent to which kids absorb such stressors, especially when parents are having trouble handling the load themselves. Be aware that chronic stress taxes family resources, possibly leading to more fragile interpersonal relationships.

The family needs to be safe so that kids can make little forays out from it with confidence, testing their wings.

If parents are depressed, as was the case with Barry Loukaitis's mother, they need to get help and not lean on their kids for support or place them in parenting roles. That was what happened with a boy I'll call Andy. He was a handsome young man but didn't date much. At school he mostly kept to himself. There was one girl, Jenny, whom he sort of liked, but Andy was afraid to talk to her. She was always kind and smiled at him in the hall, so Andy thought often of asking her on a date but just couldn't get up the nerve. He talked to his mother about what he should do, and she advised that he forget about her. After all, he was too busy with school work, and he "didn't need to be distracted by some girl."

Nevertheless, Andy kept hoping he'd develop the courage to ask Jenny on a date. When the opportunity came, he went for it. To his amazement, Jenny agreed to go. That weekend, he nervously prepared for his big night out. As he was walking out the door to pick up Jenny, his mom began to cry. Andy stepped back into the house and asked what was wrong.

"Nothing. Go."

But the crying persisted, and Andy was torn. His mother had a history of depression and had been in and out of hospitals. Each episode began with crying spells.

Once again, Andy felt responsible. He called Jenny and regrettably canceled the date. Jenny understood. He walked into the room and sat with his mom.

"I feel better now, son," she said. "You didn't have to cancel your date. I know you wanted to go. But I didn't want to be alone tonight. I'm afraid of what may happen. Thank you."

Unrightfully so, Andy carried the burden of his mother's sadness. She leaned on him for support and placed him in a terrible position. She wanted him to take care of her.

We need to be so careful not to do this to our children. When we dump stress on our teen, we sap his or her energy for creative pursuits. The family needs to be safe so that kids can make little forays out from it with confidence, testing their wings. As Edith Schaeffer says:

> The family should be the place where each new human being can have an early atmosphere conducive to the development of constructive creativity. Parents, aunts and uncles, grandparents, and sisters and brothers can squash, stamp out, ridicule, and demolish the first attempts at creativity, and continue this demolition long enough to cripple spontaneous outbursts of creation. These things can take place carelessly, and we might be astonished at what we have unconsciously spoiled. [3]

One good way to reduce stress and keep the creative juices flowing in your kids is to keep rules consistent and predictable. Then kids have a sense of freedom for other pursuits. Structure is already there; environmental chaos won't reign. So, for example, if you say you're going to do something, follow through. In a time of overwhelming hormonal changes, kids desperately need external structure and understanding to reduce their internal stress.

Variable #2: How well do we support one another around here?

Family support is crucial in maintaining a teen's mental health. In the past decades, teens could talk with extended family members for additional support. Today, relatives often live far away, leaving teens feeling more isolated. In the absence of extended families, youth may turn to peers to fill a gaping nurture void.

When family members are incapable of supporting one another during the high stress of adolescence, breakdown occurs. Adolescent support needs include:

- Love, caring and respect, which builds esteem.

- Affirmation, which validates thoughts and feelings as normal.

- Concrete actions that assist kids in managing their world.

Family support is linked to a child's ability to develop effective coping responses as well. This means that early in a child's development the family teaches a child how to cope with internal negative feelings and external difficult situations. For example, in the case of many of the shooters, these teens showed a lack of appropriate external coping responses for their internal pain. Consistent, ongoing support at home makes all the difference to a teen. And choosing to fill a home with love and encouragement is a critical parenting responsibility:

> Your home can be a place for dying or living, for wilting or blooming, for anxiety or peace, for discouragement or affirmation, for criticism or approval, for profane disregard or reverence, for suspicion or trust, for blame or forgiveness, for alienation or closeness, for violation or respect, for carelessness or caring. By your daily choices, you will make your home what you want it to be. [4]

Variable #3: Do we know what our teens are doing at all times?

Parental awareness has been questioned repeatedly in the news reports of the high school shootings. Without casting blame, I do want to state clearly: We parents need to know what our children are doing, with whom they hang out, who the parents of their friends are, what those parents stand for and what those teens listen to, read, watch and do. Does it sound rather daunting? It is. Nevertheless, we have to know in order to intervene.

While teens holler, "Give me some privacy!", we need to monitor and supervise their activities. Too many parents take a passive role, feeling overwhelmed by the constant badgering, giving in to baleful pleadings under pressure and generally not standing firm on limits and standards of behavior. No, we can't be our teen's best friend. That may come later in life. For now, we must be the parent—laying down the rules, checking on behavior, demanding accountability.

We parents need to know what our children are doing, with whom they hang out, who the parents of their friends are, what those parents stand for and what those teens listen to, read, watch and do.

We simply can't afford to be afraid of our teenagers. If we're afraid of them, think of how afraid they must be of their own impulses. Teens want power but can't always handle it. They're still in the process of separating and differentiating from their families of origin. So find out whom your kids emulate. Who are their role models? Whom do they admire? Whose pictures or posters grace their notebooks, walls, wallets and clothing? If they're gradually growing up and moving away from their family, as they should, whom are they moving toward?

Variable #4: How well are we communicating?

The best way to engage your teens in conversation is to ask them about themselves and what they think about. Value their opinions. Keep an open mind, but don't be afraid to differ with their views. Just differ in a way that doesn't put them on the defensive. Because of their development, they need more input in family decisions, and parents need to use more negotiation skills in setting rules and boundaries. Maintain open channels of communication by listening, seeking kids out even when they avoid you, giving them space when they need it and choosing your battles wisely.

One key point here is to remember to avoid shaming language. Avoid using put-downs, projecting blame or attacking the self-esteem of your teenager. When they express emotions, don't ridicule or turn them off. When they share ideas that upset you, listen and don't interrupt. Dialogue with your teen instead of preaching.

Variable #5: Do we resolve our conflicts in healthy ways?

Interpersonal conflict does occur in families. How it is handled is a learning lab for children. They watch when their parents disagree to see how the family handles someone not getting his or her own way. Implicitly or explicitly, conflict resolution is taught—good ways, bad ways or no way at all.

Kids act out in the world what they have learned at home. If they know how to handle conflict positively, that skill will transfer to other relationships. If not, they may choose to act violently when faced with conflict.

Variable # 6: Do we have a good structure for discipline in this home?

Appropriate, loving discipline is a key factor in raising healthy kids. Taking an extreme approach, whether it is too permissive or too rigid, should be avoided. When discipline is too permissive, kids are unmonitored, unsupervised, lack boundaries and have the potential to get into trouble. At its worst, permissive discipline puts kids in harm's way.

One of the best resources we give our kids is "us," which means we spend time with them.

When I was a teen, I had a best friend. I always thought her family was so cool. They had this great house for entertaining, stayed up long hours partying and never paid much attention to their daughter. My family, on the other hand, had to know where I was at all times, gave me curfews and always had at least one parent at home. That's why I was surprised by something my friend said one night when we were eating ice cream on the lawn of her back yard. She told me she thought it was great that my parents were so involved and kept tabs on me. She looked quite sad, and I asked if she would like that from her parents, too. She said, "Yes, it would make me feel safe."

In the cases of Eric Harris and Dylan Klebold, *Time* magazine commentator Amy Dickinson aptly raises these questions regarding parental involvement:

Is it possible for parents to miss homicidal rage? Where were the Harrises and Klebolds when their sons were watching *Natural Born Killers* over and over? Have the parents seen that movie? Have they ever played Doom and the other blood-soaked computer games that occupied their children? Did these "educated professionals" take a look at the hate-filled website their kids created? Were the Harrises aware of the pipe-bomb factory that was in their two-car garage? The kid down the street was aware of it, and he's 10 years old. [5]

Again, I have said that the blame for evil lies solely with evildoers. Yet we as parents are responsible to know effective discipline strategies for teens and to use them. This involves awareness of wrongdoing and readiness to take action against it.

Of course, discipline strategies change with the developmental stages of a child. It's not appropriate to spank a sixteen-year-old! Likewise, what works with one sibling may not work with another. Adapt your discipline strategy to the personality of each teen. Some examples of appropriate disciplinary strategies are: 1) specify that certain behaviors earn the right to drive the car, use the phone, go out with friends; 2) negotiate more rules instead of dictating them; and 3) use contracts to spell out conditions in writing.

One of the best resources we give our kids is "us," which means we spend time with them. Perhaps we need to rethink dual-career parenting, which takes both parents out of the home and leaves kids alone and unsupervised for hours. Teens may appear grown up and able to handle that responsibility, but emotionally they still need our guidance. Remember, developmentally they are still learning judgment, problem-solving and relating skills. The importance of your presence is that you give immediate feedback to situations as they occur. Hands-on nurturing has no substitute.

The beauty of good discipline is that it provides structure. Teens need plenty of rest, regular nutritious meals and a realistic schedule. Left to their own means this won't happen. They grab fast food and stay up late. They often take on too much and overload their schedules. Parents and kids together must negotiate rules and discuss the consequences for lack of self-care.

On the other hand, overly rigid discipline can foster anger and rebellion. When parents can't respond to the unique needs of their kids, and only enforce inflexible rules, kids find ways to resist, either in passive or active forms. Many passive-aggressive kids are secretly angry at overly rigid parents, and they act out their anger in ways that hurt others. In particular, parents who have unrealistic expectations or abuse their children set the stage for possible acting out.

Obviously, the best discipline balances both responsible independence and realistic rules. Families that are flexible, cohesive and effectively manage conflict do the best.

Variable #7: Are we good parent role models?

Mothers and fathers are so important, but here let me

focus on the father's role. I can't stress enough the importance of dads in the lives of their sons. Sons learn how to be men from their dads. The absentee father communicates "You are not important" to a son. Fathers who are consumed with work or other interests, spending long hours away from their families, pay a heavy price indeed. They are disconnected, uninvolved and often unaware of their sons' emotions, interests, behaviors, friends or struggles. As a result, lost fathers beget lost boys.

Fathers who attempt to shame their boys into manhood create just the opposite—boys who are angry, lost, confused and in pain. Fathers who never cry in front of their sons and don't permit it—who tease and ridicule their boys—who push them beyond their physical or emotional capabilities, raise boys filled with shame and rage.

So gentlemen, be a positive role model for every boy you know. Avoid using addictive substances, lashing out with bad language, showing disrespect toward others and making prejudicial slurs. Boys are looking on!

> Boys become men by watching men, by standing close to men. Manhood is a ritual passed from generation to generation with precious few spoken instructions. Passing the torch of manhood is a fragile, tedious task. If the right of passage is successfully completed, the boy-become-man is like an oak of hardwood character. His shade and influence will bless all those who are fortunate enough to lean on him and rest under his canopy.[6]

Kids do what parents do, not what they say. Walk your talk and make it wholesome. They also watch and imitate how you handle pain and anger. As parents, you are the primary model for lovingkindness in relationships.

In contrast, have you ever considered that abusive fathers actually model violence? Physical abuse not only harms a child but teaches him to handle feelings by hitting others. Most of our prisons are filled with men who are violent. These are men, not boys, who rape, steal, kill and beat women. Even with the high-profile case of O. J. Simpson, domestic violence continues in our families as a model for young boys to deal with anger and feelings of inferiority.

Abuse is terribly destructive in all its forms. Sexual abuse violates children's physical boundaries, creates shame and uses them as powerless objects. Anger and rage are common responses to this type of abuse. Verbal abuse wears on the self-esteem of a child. Constant criticism, yelling and violent threats tear at a son's identity, creating pain that sets the stage for possible destructive behavior later.

Typically these forms of abuse are passed down through the generations. God warned us:

> I the LORD thy God am a jealous God, visiting the iniquity of the fathers upon the children unto the third and fourth generation of them that hate me.
> —EXODUS 20:5, KJV

Variable #8: Have we taught our children biblical values?

Here we come to the importance of moral and spiritual guidance in the home. Parents are responsible for giving their children a faith perspective for life. They teach their children right from wrong and impart values. Without a moral and spiritual framework, children flounder in a postmodern culture that reduces absolute truth to mere relativism. Instead of learning universal truth from parents, kids end up creating subjective "virtual realities" in which their point of view is all that matters. As

Without a moral and spiritual framework, children flounder in a postmodern culture that reduces absolute truth to mere relativism.

a result, biblical models of morality are replaced by cultural pop icons who often preach immorality. Our lax and sometimes nonexistent teaching in this area leaves kids vulnerable to the influences of the larger culture.

Yet we can paddle upstream and fight the cultural current. Here's how one man used a simple, everyday situation as a teachable moment:

> My son wanted to help change a flat tire on my car. He couldn't loosen the lug nuts. He ran out of energy to unscrew them all. He couldn't lift the old tire off or put the new one

on. Once the new tire was on, he tried to get away with only putting on every other lug nut. It took twice as long with his help.

While he couldn't help me as much as he thought he could, he went away thinking he had helped me more than he did. The experience made a large spiritual impression on him. His self-esteem grew by a mile, and now he understands the concepts of diligence and excellence in a deeper way. Those are biblical values, and I impressed them upon my son in a way that was natural, not contrived. I wasn't teaching him how to change a flat tire; I was teaching him how to be a man of God.[7]

Teach your teen the eternal values in everything you do. There are moral absolutes your family needs to know and act upon. Don't get caught up in the relativism of our culture.

> You must commit yourselves wholeheartedly to these commands I am giving you today. Repeat them again and again to your children. Talk about them when you are at home and when you are away on a journey, when you are lying down and when you are getting up again.
> —DEUTERONOMY 6:6–7

Finally, pray and intercede for your teen daily. Your teen needs your prayer covering. Ask God for wisdom as a parent and for your teen to make wise decisions. So many people credit a praying parent or relative for seeing them through tough times.

Variable #9: Do we know what our kids are doing with their peer groups?

Remember that in adolescent development, peers play an increasingly important role. Prior to adolescence, parents may have had more influence in a child's decision making. One hopes that the influence will be lasting, but peers present a new challenge.

Participation in a peer group that sanctions and rewards violence makes violence more likely to occur. This is why parents need to know to what peer groups their children belong and what they espouse and act out.

According to reports, peers at their high school inflicted severe emotional pain on Eric and Dylan, to which they responded with more and more violent ideation and actions. Peer groups need to recognize the impact of their words and actions on kids outside

Tell your teen often, "I love you."

their cliques. Because of the fragility of adolescent identities, exclusion often leaves deep wounds.

> "Kids who feel powerless and rejected are capable of doing horrible things," reflects professor Larry Brendtro. Listen to the viewpoint of a high school student: "If you go to school, and people make fun of you every day, and you don't have friends, it drives you to insanity."[8]

In essence, the jocks' clique had contributed to the creation of the Trench Coat Mafia. Eric and Dylan's response came when they entered the library, laughing excitedly, "Who's next? All the jocks stand up. We're going to kill every one of you."[9] This clearly represents the worst outcome of destructive peer pressure.

Variable #10: Do we love one another unconditionally?

God offers conditional love; His model is clear. "We love because he first loved us" (1 John 4:19, NIV). God's unconditional love gives grace and forgiveness, empowers us to be all He has created us to be and moves us toward a more intimate walk with Him. The challenge for family members is to do the same for one another, constantly showing unconditional love.

So tell your teen often, "I love you." Merely showing love with your hard work or gifts is not enough. Verbalize your feelings of love every day, so there's no question where you stand in the mind of your teenager. Your teen must feel your love *in a way that means love to her*. This is the way to encourage the blossoming of your child's full potential. In this regard, I recall what well-known youth leader Ron Luce has said:

> You may see your teen writing notes in youth group or making spit wads in church. He may fight with his brothers and sisters at home. You may wonder how your teen could change the world when you can't even get him to change his sheets. God sees all that stuff, too, yet He still believes in his potential—and He is still counting on him.

Relational Pain: From the Roots Up

Our young people need to know we have discovered the seeds of greatness within them. When they finally find someone who recognizes their potential, they will abandon the direction this world has given them. When they see an older generation that is convinced of their potential, there is nothing they won't do to fulfill that potential.[10]

Isn't that a wonderful way to describe the future of our younger generations? The future is bright if families can build strong foundations that keep the roots of interpersonal pain at bay. So begin to think about these areas in your own family. Here's a quick and easy way to rate your family on these ten points. Put an "x" on each line on the chart to indicate where your family is. Then discuss your insights together!

Family Stress

Low   High

Parental Awareness

Ignorant   Informed

Family Support

Low   High

Communication

Lousy   Good

KIDS KILLING KIDS

Interpersonal Conflict

Avoid	Address appropriately	Combative

Discipline

Permissive	Balanced	Rigid

The Father Quotient

Absent	Involved	Abusive

Moral and Spiritual Guidance

Absent	Very strong

Influence of Peer Pressure

Low	Balanced	High

Unconditional Love

Never	Always

Handling the Hurt

If you will diligently attempt to analyze your family within the categories above, and become aware of your family's unique vulnerabilities, you'll deal successfully with the pain that naturally flows into every family. Blessings upon you in all your attempts to build a loving family! And now I leave you with a few parting words of advice, some ways to prevent the pain from becoming violence . . .

Spend time with your teenager.

He may act as if he doesn't want to be with you, but he does. Ask your teen what he wants to do, then do it. How about: Go to his school events. Take him fishing. Develop a hobby together. Read Scripture and pray together. Work together on a project. Talk about the local news and world events. Be vulnerable. Share your feelings, your successes and failures.

Get to know your neighbors.

Engage them as helpful sources of information. They need to partner with you in knowing what the kids in your neighborhood are doing. When a neighbor sees your teen misbehaving, they need the freedom to tell you without you becoming defensive. This may be hard for you, but work on it! Likewise, if you see their teen misbehaving, tell them in a nice way.

Meet with their teachers.

If your teen is having academic or behavioral problems, talk with his teachers or counselors. Maintain continual contact until the problems are resolved. Teachers are busy and may not be receptive to your questions. Persist. Don't give up.

Build self-esteem.

Every kid achieves at something! Self-esteem grows as we give kids opportunities to demonstrate their competence and trustworthiness. That means having tasks to accomplish and responsibilities to carry out. Then notice what your teen does right, and comment on it. Don't focus on failure. Build on his successes.

Set realistic expectations.

Unrealistic expectations may create a teen who is anxious, perfectionistic, frustrated or who gives up. On the other hand, mere praise can't build self-esteem; praise for a job well done certainly can.

Build a support network.

Internally, family members need to be supportive of each other. You also need external support from other families, church groups and others. Also, get professional help when you need it. Don't allow the perceived stigma of seeking mental health services or counseling stop you from receiving the help you need. If you're having problems with work, parenting, marriage or relationships, and can't fix them on your own, ask someone to help you. Likewise, encourage any family member who is not functioning well to get outside help.

Deal with family estrangement.

Don't ignore relational problems, whether they are parent-child, parent-parent or generational. This means reconciling differences between immediate and extended family members and forgiving offenses.

Stop abuse of all kinds.

Anyone who suspects or witnesses abuse is required by law to report it. If someone in your family is abusive, get help.

Help your teen find a place to belong.

Too many teens feel isolated and left out. Seek out youth groups, interest groups and extracurricular activity groups that your teen will enjoy.

All families face interpersonal pain. We can't always control our circumstances or what others do, but we can control how we respond to our hurts. Without the Lord and a spiritual foundation, it's extremely difficult to take the steps that bring healing. But by His grace, we can become Christlike models for our teens.

In the Lord we are overcomers of our past—more than conquerors. We are victors, not victims. As parents we can show the way, and with the power of the Holy Spirit within us, we can be Jesus to our kids.

As parents we can show the way, and with the power of the Holy Spirit within us, we can be Jesus to our kids.

> And I am convinced that nothing can ever separate us from his love. Death can't, and life can't. The angels can't, and the demons can't. Our fears for today, our worries about tomorrow, and even the powers of hell can't keep God's love away. Whether we are high above the sky or in the deepest ocean, nothing in all creation will ever be able to separate us from the love of God that is revealed in Christ Jesus our Lord.
>
> —ROMANS 8:38–39

Dear God, the seeds of my past seem to blossom in all I do. Please weed out the early, bad influences that have made me thoughtless or uncaring as an adult. Let me take hold of the good that keeps flowing toward me from Your heart—and may I pass it on to the next young person I see.

4

Get in touch with your gun-toting, testosterone-pumping, cold-blooded murdering side.

—Ad for a Sony video game [1]

Everything we're exposed to influences us. These [violent] films influence us, and the TV programs we see influence us. The weaker your family is, the more they influence you. The problems with families in our cities are catastrophic, but when you put violent programs [before] people who haven't had a lot of love in their lives, who are angry anyway, it's like pouring gasoline on the fire.

—Ted Turner [2]

Cultural Pain: Media Influences

Has something like this ever been your story? Turning on the tube for some late-night diversion, you flip to the Nickleodean Channel and settle in for a couple of lighthearted half-hours with Lucy, Ricky, Fred and Ethel. Then you wind down the evening with a heartwarming episode featuring Rob and Laura. The plot line: Rob has been ordered to put together a funny sketch for his TV show—by tomorrow morning. But will his hard-driving boss like his ideas? The tension builds . . .

After enough of *I Love Lucy* and *The Dick Van Dyke Show* to sufficiently relax your mind, as you sleepily walk down the hall and head for bed, it hits you: *How nice not to have seen any blood.* Imagine—an hour and a half of television viewing . . and not one beating, shooting, stabbing or rape. Not even an obscene word.

Nice.

And as you snuggle down into the covers, it may occur to you that the most violent event in any of those mindless minutes of your little foray into TV heaven was this: Rob, once again, tripped over that silly-looking ottoman in the living room.

What Ever Happened to Ozzie and Harriet?

Compare Rob's harmless pratfall to a recurrent theme on the Comedy Channel's *South Park* cartoon show. It's a running gag, too—"Who killed Kenny?" In almost every episode, the youngster gets killed afresh, over and over again.

It's supposed to be hilarious.

Sadly, it's becoming a common theme in our culture, almost defining the essence of our entertainment environment these days: violence for the fun of it. Clearly, June and Ward Cleaver live far, far in the past.

There's no doubt in my mind that we must wake up to the barrage of violence blaring into our living rooms, night after night. Whether it's violence for fun or down-and-dirty mayhem for the pure shock value, so many of our TV programs are hurting us, dragging our entire society down to barbaric levels. Just consider some of the alarming statistics—even from a decade ago!

- An average of 9.5 violent acts per hour appeared on prime time TV in 1989–90.

- Saturday morning network programming featured twenty violent acts per hour in 1989–90.

- By the age of eighteen, a typical child has witnessed an estimated two hundred thousand acts of violence, including twenty-five thousand murders on TV.[3]

If it was that bad ten years ago, think of what it's like today. Do we really want all of this violence? A 1993 survey in *Electronic Media* magazine revealed that 74 percent of TV station managers agreed that TV is too violent. They favored voluntary network reduction in violence levels and warnings.[4] We do, too, right?

But why is TV violence nevertheless so prevalent? Perhaps it has to do with the wrong answer to this hotly debated question: *Does TV violence lead to aggression?*

Here's the right answer: *Yes!*

Although highly debated in the popular press, the scientific community has gathered a mountain of evidence to support this conclusion. Leonard Eron, professor emeritus of the University of Illinois at Chicago, succinctly summarizes this relationship:

> There can no longer be any doubt that heavy exposure to televised violence is one of the causes of aggressive behavior, crime and violence in society. The evidence comes from both the laboratory and real-life studies. Television violence affects youngsters of all ages, of both genders, at all socioeconomic levels and all levels of intelligence. The effect is not limited to children who are already disposed to being aggressive and is not restricted to this country. The fact that we get this same

finding of a relation between television violence and aggression in children in study after study, in one country after another, cannot be ignored.[5]

Other psychological research reveals that TV violence can have these effects on children and teens: [6]

- May engage in copycat violence
- Are stimulated to commit impulsive, aggressive acts
- Learn violent ways to resolve conflicts
- Are desensitized to real-life violence
- See the world as scary and mean
- Expect others to be violent

Most researchers agree that TV violence has these three overall effects on kids:

1. Aggressive behavior

Specific qualities increase the likelihood that a teen will identify with an aggressor. Identification increases when the aggressor is attractive, justifies violent behavior, uses weapons, is graphic and realistic, is rewarded and the violence is presented in a humorous way.

2. Fearful attitudes

Fear is enhanced when the victims are attractive, the objects of unjustified violence and are portrayed in realistic and graphic manner. Fear is also increased when the aggressors are rewarded. Research indicates that in 73 percent of all TV violent scenes the perpetrators go unpunished.[7] Also, when younger kids believe that TV violence is real, it affects their actions as well as their attitudes. They tend to believe that the world is unsafe, that violence is an appropriate way to deal with problems and that violence is glamorous with few consequences.

3. Desensitization

The more teens are exposed to violent events, the more desensitized to violence they become. Long-term studies indicate that exposure to violence lessens sensitivity to the pain and suffering of others, increases fear of the real world, leads to aggression toward others and normalizes aggression. One educator, writing in a local newspaper, was shocked by the level of desensitization in her students:

> I often turn off the television during supper time due to the gory pictures on the evening news. On the other hand, kids anticipate, expect and laud violent scenes. While describing a violent accident to my middle school students last year, I was met with: "Cool, neat . . . how much blood was on his face . . . ?" I was shocked by their callous comments.[8]

And listen to what Chris Haley, a seventeen-year-old junior at Lewisville High School in Lewisville, Texas, has to say:

Our generation is far more desensitized to violence than any other generation. TVs raise children now more than parents do, and television caters to children's violent fantasies. Parents are working more and spending less time with their kids.[9]

TV violence appears to influence both the attitudes and behaviors of kids at risk. Some kids identified at risk are those with emotional disturbances, learning disabilities, abused and in families with high stress levels.[10] They tend to identify with violent heroes, fantasize and repeatedly think about violent programs and find the means to commit physical acts of violence.

TV violence appears to influence both the attitudes and behaviors of kids at risk.

We also know that the effects of TV violence increase for teenage boys and decrease dramatically for teenage girls.[11] Keep in mind that teens process information differently, depending on a number of variables, including their life experiences, age, amount of TV viewing, belief that TV is real and intellectual achievement.

While TV violence may be only one contributor to an already at-risk child, we cannot ignore the impact of this medium. We do know that TV viewing falls off somewhat as the adolescent gets older because he or she becomes more interested in pop music. Music speaks more to the themes of adolescence—independence, sexuality, romance. In fact, many teens consider TV to be the parents' medium. Television is a passive activity requiring low concentration and does not engage a teen's emerging thinking and feeling abilities.

What practical guidelines can we put into play in trying to safeguard our kids from TV violence? Consider these four:

Viewing Guideline #1:
Begin teaching discernment at the earliest possible moment.

In keeping with the stage of your child's development, as soon as he's interested in television viewing, teach him to choose shows that are also compatible with Christian values. Of course, in early childhood you'll choose for your child when and what he watches. Cartoons may be filled with violence, for instance. Carefully monitor which shows your young children watch, especially on Saturday morning and on cable channels that feature cartoons.

Naturally, you won't want to resort to the TV for babysitting your children. Instead, be there to ask questions about what they're watching: Which characters behave well or poorly, and why? What morality is being taught by this show? Is that family like our family? Why? Do those kids behave differently from you? Is their behavior right or wrong? The idea here is to develop a partnership with your kid. Talking with an adult gives kids alternative ways to think about as they view the show.

Be sure to view shows with your teens, too. Know what they're watching so you can meaningfully discuss the show's content and values. If the show contains undesirable content, explain to your teen why it's not appropriate viewing material. Be certain to keep any criticism of TV programming focused on the content and not on your teen, however. Then encourage teens to express their opinions. Let them analyze the show. Invite them to review the content and tell you why it's worthwhile. That way, you're teaching them to think critically about what they watch.[12]

Viewing Guideline #2:
Decide what violence you may condone.

First, parents need to take a personal inventory regarding their own beliefs about violence. Examine how tolerant and desensitized you may have become over the years. Then eliminate programs that promote "violence for fun." One of the most startling reports about the shooters was that they laughed as they killed people. Yet violence is hardly funny. Also eliminate programs that promote rape myths. (Rape is always about violence— not primarily sexual—and treats women as objects. We have no business exposing our children to this stuff.)

Realize that not all programs that contain violence are the same. Some violence may come through in the news or historical war documentaries that educate, but they can still have a negative effect. Parents and teens must decide together what constitutes suitable viewing, so talk directly talk to your teen about the *realities* of violence, clearly distinguishing between reality and fantasy. I've already established that TV rarely shows the real consequences of violence. Therefore, it's our responsibility to teach our teens the consequences. In addition, we can teach problem-solving alternatives to violence. Television can be a springboard for teaching your kids new strategies to handle specific situations and for introducing them to biblical values.

Viewing Guideline #3:
Screen the shows that come into your home—and be willing to turn the TV off if "nothing good is on."

Turn off the TV if it's upsetting or agitating your young child or teen. "Television may be the only electrical appliance that's more useful after it's turned off," said one educator. Discuss with your teen the reasons for doing this.

It's virtually impossible to eliminate all programs on TV that contain some violence, though some families do so by not having a TV. But if you choose to have television, then the family must abide by certain guidelines. How much TV viewing should be allowed? Experts recommend two hours a day (and that's a lot).

Finally, use your TV guide or a Christian guide like *Movieguide* to select your programs. The key is to be proactive rather than reactive. Also use your VCR, which is great for screening programs ahead of time or even reviewing a program after your child has seen it. Or simply find alternative media. Christian television, public TV and radio, magazines, newspapers and certain cable channels can be excellent alternatives.

Viewing Guideline #4:
Don't use television as a substitute for family relationships at night.

Find meaningful things your family can do together in addition to watching TV. Turn off the TV at dinner time and talk together as a family instead. It's hard to have conversations with other family members with the TV blaring, not to mention what the content might be.

In fact, why not turn off the TV whenever possible? Cancel your subscription to cable channels that show violence or premium channels that you find objectionable. And finally, be sure to take the TV out of your teen's room and any isolated places in your home. There's just no way to monitor what and how much teens are watching when a TV set is hiding in their own room.

Having completed this quick roller-coaster ride through the world of TV violence, it's time to turn our attention to the other forms of media that promote a culture of cruelty in our midst. We'll deal with the movies, pop music, computer-video games and the Internet, in turn. Hold on for a violent ride . . .

The Wonderful World of Movies—NOT!

Movies, as with television, portray graphic and realistic acts of violence. The difference is that the huge screen and its surround-sound partner bring pulse-pounding action images closer to home in more disturbing ways. The large size of the images (and the often overly loud crashings and explodings) somehow imprints scenes on our psyches.

I'm not sure how you react to all of this, but in my case, I see the immediate effects on my family. Disney's kid movies, for example, created so many problems for my son that we hardly see them anymore. He was terrified by the opening scene in *Aladdin* in which a large, occultic symbol arose out of the ground. We had to walk out of *The Hunchback of Notre Dame* when they tied up Esmeralda to burn her at the stake. And my son pleaded to leave during the opening scene of *Pocahontas* because the violent storm frightened him. The larger-than-life images and THX sound overwhelmed his senses. At eight years old, he knows what many adults don't—he can't handle the violence, nor should he have to!

Kids must be taught at an early age how to become a media discerner.

The nonbiblical morality, lack of respect for other human beings and violent themes of today's movies are constantly discussed in our home as we talk about why they are inappropriate for viewing. When your children become teens, you can no longer screen every movie they see. So kids must be taught at an early age how to become a media discerner. We have to live in this world and cannot shelter them from every evil or harmful thing. But we can teach them how to set limits, and we can try our best to prevent destructive influences from entering their minds.

Scripture reminds us that the righteous cannot "listen to those who plot murder," and must "shut their eyes to all enticement to do wrong" (Isa. 33:15). Our teens cannot fill their minds with violence and expect no ill effects. Instead of taking in movie violence, the alternative must be to fix their thoughts on what is righteous. The Bible instructs:

> Fix your thoughts on what is true and honorable and right. Think about things that are pure and lovely and admirable. Think about things that are excellent and worthy of praise.
>
> —PHILIPPIANS 4:8

The subject of the influence of movie violence has been raised repeatedly by commentators on the high school shootings. These folks do have a point. Let's look a little closer at four of the movies to get a good idea of the themes they offered as "entertainment."

The Basketball Diaries. Recall that the Paducah shooter, Michael Carneal, watched this movie, which stars teen heartthrob Leonardo DiCaprio. When asked by authorities if he saw the movie, Michael responded that he remembered the fantasy scene in which the lead character shoots his classmates and teachers while wearing a black trench coat. In a similar fashion, Michael shot those at his school. In fact, according to a report by *ABC News,* "During pretrial investigation of the crime, Carneal specifically cited *The Basketball Diaries* scene as the model for his actions."[13] The movie chronicles how a basketball athlete turns to drugs and violence out of a feeling of alienation from peers and family. This film overflows with explicitly raw and morbid scenes of sex, addiction and death. The fantasy killing scene of the main character wearing a trench coat concealing his automatic weapon was apparently replayed for real in the Columbine High School shootings, as well.

Natural Born Killers. This Oliver Stone movie was a favorite viewing pastime of the Littleton shooters and shooter Barry Loukaitis. Reportedly, Barry bragged about the great fun it would be to go on a killing spree. In the film, the main character comes from an abusive family and engages in vulgar dialogue and taboo subjects. The verbally abusive father treats women as objects. The main character, Mallory, believes that morality has no meaning. In an attempt to escape her pain, Mallory murders her parents and announces to her brother that he is free. The background soundtracks roar with applause.

The Doors. Several years ago, I noticed a number of teens showing up for therapy with the picture of Jim Morrison and and his rock band The Doors on their T-shirts. Intrigued with how this generation revived the music of The Doors, I asked the kids about Morrison's life. Their answers? "He was awesome! Deep!" But he was morbid, depressed and suicidal, too. A few years later Oliver Stone made a movie about Jim Morrison's life aptly called *The Doors*. I went to see it to understand more.

Val Kilmer's portrayal of Jim was frightening. This movie documented the hellish descent into Jim's self-destruction, including occultic and suicidal involvement. In one scene, Jim holds a knife over his heart and pleads with his girlfriend to kill him. I could hardly handle it and should have walked out. Later that night, tormented by the movie scenes, I woke my husband and asked him to pray over me. I felt oppressed and couldn't shake the images. I spent half the night praying and speaking the name of Jesus.

The Matrix. This 1999 science fiction hit depicts the hero, played by actor Keanu Reeves, dressed in a Goth black trench coat, adorned with multiple firearms and killing huge numbers of law enforcement types. The film infuses the viewers with heavy doses of doom, gloom and grunge.

Like many Americans, I saw the Academy Award-winning *Saving Private Ryan*. I almost left the theater during the first ten minutes because I could barely endure the rapid-pace intensity of the killing. With tears and gut-wrenching grief, I leaned over to my husband, closed my eyes and whispered, "Make it stop. Please make it stop. I can't take it!" These violent, graphic, visual images were unshakable and overwhelming, even for me—a therapist who has spent hundreds of hours listening to the post-traumatic stress of patients. And, of course, we were viewing the realities of a real war.

During the scene in which a mother was told her sons were killed, I flashed back to a few years ago when an Army officer knocked on my door at home, holding a telegram saying that my brother was missing (and later announced dead) from a plane explosion. Again, I was sobbing, and my heart was pounding as I repeated, "Make it stop. Please make it stop." The power of the filmmaker's visual images cannot be underestimated. I was reacting from a mature, adult perspective and was still struggling with the intensity.

Here's my point, however: At the end of *Saving Private Ryan*, I stumbled out of the theater, numb and speechless. Yet behind me, three teens and two preteens were pushing forward ahead of me. I overhead them saying, "Cool! I loved it. Wasn't the killing scene great!" They were laughing—not crying—and punching each other.

I was so disturbed. All I could think was, *Lord, what is wrong with us?*

We are all disturbed by what we see, and at times feel powerless to stop the madness. Author and novelist John Grisham was quoted as saying:

> The last hope of imposing some sense in
> Hollywood will come through the great
> American tradition, the lawsuit. It will take a
> large verdict against the likes of Oliver Stone,
> and then the party will be over.

While I understand the truth in this statement, I believe it will take more than a huge lawsuit to reverse the downward trend in our culture. It will take a change in heart, a turning of our ways, a transformation by Jesus Christ in us. It will take prayer. Lots of prayer, intercessory prayer. God loves the makers of these movies as much as He loves you and me. Let's pray for their souls, for it is His will that none should perish.

Take a moment to review the guidelines related to television violence, and then take these additional steps as you decide what movies and videos your family will see:

- Pay attention to ratings, but don't use them as your only criteria.

- Read reviews about the movies in advance.

- Know what movies your teens and their friends are going to see.

- Know what videos they are renting (or their friends are renting).

- Talk with your teens about the movies they have already seen; they may still need to debrief.

- Preview movies that are questionable.

- Go with your teens to watch certain movies. Then discuss them.

- Always model good viewing habits yourself.

Postmodern Music: A Violent Connection

Although we have no direct proof that violent lyrics beget violent teens, researchers imply the connections. Psychologist David Elkind remarks, "Music can influence as much as any visual media." Intuitively, we sense that there must be some kind of connection between certain kinds of music and kids at risk. Teens spend a lot of time listening to music—approximately four to six hours a day. Listening to music has always been a normal part of teen culture. What's changing is the amount of violence contained in today's lyrics.

As in all other forms of media, music has become more markedly violent. When I think about the words in songs of the 1960s, like the Beatles' song "I Want to Hold Your Hand," I realize that such a simple, innocent sentiment is a far cry from the pounding, sensual, four-letter, raw gansta raps that say, "I wanna f _ _ _ you." And the lyrics from the '60s are light years removed from Marilyn Manson, who is known to make statements such as, "Who said date rape isn't kind?" or "The housewife I will beat" or "I slit my teenage wrist."

MTV and VH-1 now allow us not only to listen to violent and antisocial lyrics but also to watch them acted out in stunning color. Again, the continual pounding of violent music messages desensitizes kids to acts of violence. Interestingly, music industry statistics reveal that 80 percent of older teens watch MTV. These kids are constantly exposed to such groups as Nine Inch Nails, who sing, using explicit profanity, that nothing can stop them and their gun.[14]

Recently I tried an experiment: I watched two evenings of MTV and tried to identify the themes being promoted. I came away with these messages:

- Carry a condom and use it.

- Fashion is an expression of the sensual, the ambiguous, the core self.

- Personal experience is what matters.

- Nothing is permanent (we'll all be annihilated anyway).

- Everything is relative.

- Live for the moment.

- Be irreverent.

- Push the boundary.

- Pierce, tattoo and party!

Quite a revelation! After viewing these scenes, my immediate response was intercession. Yet remarkably, music industry officials deny music's undeniable influence on teens. President/CEO of the Recording Industry Association of America (RIAA), Hilary Rosen, intones, "In the coming days, we may find out more about the cause of this tragedy [the Littleton shooting], but we do know that music does not drive teenagers to violent despair, nor does it put guns and weapons in the hands of children. It's too easy to make music a scapegoat."[15]

Distancing himself from any possible influence over teens and violence, rocker Marilyn Manson, on April 22, 1999, issued this statement: "I have been asked to comment by numerous news organizations on the Colorado school tragedy. It's tragic and disgusting anytime young people's lives are taken in an act of senseless violence. My condolences go out to the students and their families."

It's time for us to redirect teens' interest in music to God's intention for song.

Such remarks must be framed in the context of the testimony given by a grief-stricken father testifying before the Senate in November of 1998. Raymond Kuntz sat before a Senate panel investigating the possible connections between "shock rock," crime and suicide. Kuntz's fifteen-year-old son had killed himself while listening to songs about death and the Antichrist.

Kuntz reflected how his son had showed him Marilyn Manson's CD, "Antichrist Superstar." The father testified, "I failed to recognize that my son was holding a hand grenade and it was live and it was going off in his mind."[16]

A few days after the Colorado shootings, an article by Eric Lipton appeared in the *Chicago Sun-Times* entitled, "Disturbed Shooters Weren't True Goths." Mr. Lipton went on to explain that while Eric Harris and Dylan

Klebold wore Goth-like clothing, listened to weird music and were obsessed with death, they were not "true Goths." Lipton then enlightened his readers further by saying that true Goths are obsessed with the macabre, have unkempt hair, are filled with self-loathing, are nihilistic, *but they are non-violent.* "True Goths" behave the way they do only to release tension and anxiety.

I suppose this was meant to relieve me somehow. But knowing these teens are obsessed with the dark side of life still screams warning signs to to all of us.

While Goth idol Marilyn Manson canceled his U.S. tour out of respect for the Littleton victims and reportedly blamed ignorance, hate and access to guns for the massacre, I can't help wondering if the music played a part in the ongoing desensitization of the teenage shooters.

The music that kids listen to *does* affect their attitudes and behaviors. While the research must still be done to understand the direct correlations between violent music and destructive behaviors, as adults we must provide guidance and directions to teens in this area. We want to steer them away from violent and antisocial lyrics and toward music that uplifts both soul and spirit.

As parents we complain about the violence, but who stops it? It's time for us to redirect teens' interest in music to God's intention for song. The psalmist describes how best to use music:

> Praise the LORD!
> Praise God in his heavenly dwelling;
>   praise him in his mighty heaven!
> Praise him for his mighty works;
>   praise his unequaled greatness!

> Praise him with a blast of the trumpet;
>   praise him with the lyre and harp!
> Praise him with the tambourine and
>   dancing;
>   praise him with stringed instruments and
>   flutes!
> Praise him with a clash of cymbals;
>   praise him with loud clanging cymbals.
> Let everything that lives sing praises to the
>   LORD!
> Praise the LORD!
>
> —PSALM 150

Let me suggest that you take these positive steps in evaluating the music to which your teens listen:

- Monitor and listen to their music.

- Read the lyrics of the songs to which they listen.

- Watch the music videos they watch.

- Educate yourself on the backgrounds of your teen's favorite music groups.

- Discuss objectional songs with your teen.

- Encourage your teen to listen to Christian music—there is great quality and good variety in today's Christian music market.

- Know the music to which your teen's friends listen.

- Pay attention to posters, notebooks, Web sites, tattoos and fan clubs and apparel.

- With your teen, destroy violent CDs and music videos.

- Teach your teens to ignore and delete junk e-mail.

Killer Games: In Your Home?

Interactive video and computer games have become one of the most popular forms of entertainment for teens. Around the world, video games amass staggering revenues—$18 billion annually, with over $10 billion in U.S. earnings. American kids who have video game machines play them about ninety minutes daily. And when researchers asked seventh and eighth graders to identify their preferences among the categories of video games, they responded:[17]

- Fantasy violence (32 percent)

- Sports (29 percent)

- General entertainment (20 percent)

- Human violence (17 percent)

- Educational games (2 percent)

The same study also found that boys who play violent video games tended to have lower self-concepts in the areas of academic ability, peer acceptance and behavior. Researchers raised concerns about these early adolescents as being "high-risk" for possibly linking the playing of violent video games with subsequent aggressive behavior. It's even more disturbing to realize that the newer games have more explicit depictions of violence. The player can now be more realistically involved in a virtual reality. The games Doom and Quake, which were talked about in the school shootings, are already less violent than a new game called Kingpin. The advertising copy reads: "Includes multiplayer gang bang death match for up to 16 thugs. Target specific body parts and actually see the damage done, including exit wounds."[18]

Arkansas State University psychologist David Grossman states that "point-and-shoot" video games have the same effect as military strategies used to break down a soldier's aversion to killing.[19] Furthermore, the newer games now have the player *shooting ordinary people at random* rather than employing the usual graphic, fantasy creatures or the bad guys. In other words, the teen is invited to become a virtual, killing sociopath.

So what's the purpose of these games? We are told they help teens relieve tension and anxiety. Others argue that these violent games are harmless and that teens know the difference between fantasy and reality. But I strongly reject these explanations. Along with others, I contend that, placed in the hands of unstable, at-risk teens who feel inferior and rejected, violent video games could do harm—especially those games whose chief aim is to simulate the killing of large numbers of people and the maiming or harming of others. According to reports, Harris and Klebold were obsessed with playing the violent video game Doom. Reports from other school shootings also referenced similar video games being played by the teens involved.

Unfortunately, there is a scarcity of research on

violent video games as they relate to behavior. Perhaps after these shootings, researchers will explore these possible connections further. However, the similarities between violent video games and TV would lead us to infer that teen aggression increases with play. In addition, since children are rewarded with being violent in these video games, the impact may even be greater. For example, to end the video game Postal, the player must shoot himself in the head.

The only explanation I can imagine for designing such violent video games is greed. Apparently such violence appeals to the dark side of our sinful natures. As Christians we must ask, "Why would anyone want to encourage this violence?" Scripture gives us the sobering answer:

> The thief cometh not, but for to steal, and to kill, and to destroy.
>
> —JOHN 10:10, KJV

Here are my suggestions for dealing with teens and their video games:

- Play the games, parents.

- Find out what games your teen's friends play.

- Eliminate games that are violent.

- Limit time spent playing games.

- Look for hidden violence and other related themes, such as the occult.

Cyber-Blessing ... or Sick Cesspool?

As a researcher, I am constantly amazed at the amount of information at my fingertips through the Internet. I'm convinced that at least half of the net is a great cyber-blessing. As a mom, I watch in wonder as my kids easily master computer skills and move with ease through the ether. And the Internet has brought such convenience to doing school projects! But the other half of the Internet can be pretty sickening and thoroughly addictive. For example, I now treat more men with pornography problems that arose from their Internet explorations.

Recently I conducted research for cohosting a TV series. The topic of one program was, "Can Men and Women Be Friends?" When I searched for that phrase on the Internet, I was immediately sent online to a porn site with pictures and graphic information about anal sex. All I could think about was how often teens must be confronted with the same pornographic images every day when they are innocently doing school research. Not only is pornography readily accessible, but so is violence. Sadly, both are often pictured together.

The Internet apparently played a powerful role in the life of Eric Harris. The step-by-step how-to of bomb making was easy to find. According to reports, Eric had a Web site filled with violence, and police evidently knew about his site prior to the shootings.

What might we learn from this? Realize that your teens can:

- Easily access violence and porn on the Web.

- Use the Web to research and plan violent acts.

- Learn about destructive, violent and antisocial behavior on the Web.

- Chat with and find others who will influence them in the wrong ways.

How pervasive is use of the Internet among teens? In a Time/CNN Poll of May 10, 1999:

- Eighty-two percent of teens said that they used the Internet for e-mail, chat rooms and visiting Web sites.

- Forty-four percent had visited X-rated sites or those with sexual content.

- Twenty-five percent had found information about hate groups.

- Twelve percent knew where to buy guns on the Web.

- Sixty-two percent said that their parents knew little or nothing about the Web sites they visited.

- Forty-three percent of teens' parents have no rules whatsoever about how their teens use the Internet.

Our culture is a context often filled with suffering, pain and hurt. Our teens are affected by the culture at large. The fragility of the world has been brought into our homes through various media. Daily we hear about and watch human disasters, terrorism, wars, bombings and murder. Technology brings the culture of tension and instability into our personal lives through images that disturb and desensitize our minds to violence and death. We cannot always protect and shelter our kids from cultural pain, but we can and must stand against the influences that seek to spread and normalize a culture of violence.

We know that during adolescence teens are capable of abstract thought and reasoning. Because of these skills and the developmental step of challenging authority, teens are more prone to imitate media violence, crimes and suicides. While a small percentage actually commit these acts, their actions can have horrific impact on the whole society, as witnessed in West Paducah and Littleton.

We cannot always protect and shelter our kids from cultural pain, but we can and must stand against the influences that seek to spread and normalize a culture of violence.

I realize that violence is complex and multidetermined. So, no single thing can account for violent behavior in teens. However, Sissela Bok, in her book *Mayhem:Violence As Public Entertainment*, comments, "We have introduced forms and amounts of media violence beyond anything achieved in other countries."[20] And we have data about media violence and choose to ignore it. The media continues to be irresponsible and inundate us with graphic images of death, torture and other unmentionable acts. For example, violent pornography that portrays women as wanting to be raped and punished, depicting them as dehumanized and devalued, is proliferating. Imagine the influence this can have on a teenage boy who is just discovering his sexuality.

The point is, we have the highest homicide rate in the world, and violence has risen dramatically in the U.S. in past decades. Something more than programs and gun control must be offered.

> Research shows that media violence affects children by increasing aggressiveness and antisocial behavior, increasing their fear of become victims, making them less sensitive to violence and to victims of violence and increasing their appetite for more violence in entertainment and in real life.[21]

The general state of denial that many media people continue to embrace is best evidenced by Time Warner Chairman and media mogul, Gerald Levin:

> This is the season of political opportunism. I can't help but think that television is an easy scapegoat. Where is the cry to stop the proliferation of guns? [22]

These kinds of comments remind me of adolescent

behavior—refusing to take responsibility and always blaming others. Responsibility must be laid at the feet of the media. Here's why: The recent massacre in Littleton once again causes us to ask, "How much influence does the violence in media have on our teens—and what should we do about it?"

What steps can we take to protect our children from the seductiveness of the bad part of the Internet?

- Use a filtered portal such as Crosswalk.com or a filtered server like MayberryRFD.com, cleanweb.net or afo.net on your computer.

- Monitor your teen's use of the Internet.

- Randomly download their sites visited and e-mail.

- Limit the time your teen spends on the Internet, and limit his e-mail correspondence to an approved list.

- Put the computer in a very public place in your home, somewhere where people are always walking by, screen facing into the room.

- Stand behind your teen occasionally and watch what he's doing on the Internet.

- Know that if your teen is in a chat room and begins typing numerals when you are watching, he could be alerting his partner that a parent is in the room.

- Use a service provider that allows parents to limit incoming e-mail.

- Randomly scan your teen's e-mail and know whom they are e-mailing.

- Examine incoming e-mail in order to understand what's been going out from your teen's e-mail.

- Type your kid's names or nicknames into a search engine and see what your teen is saying on his Web site and message boards—and see what others are saying.

- Tell your teen not to reveal personal information online to anyone.

- If your teen becomes addicted to the Web and will not obey your family's rules, disconnect the phone line.

But suppose you don't understand the computer well enough to know how to check on a teen? You may need to take a course and become computer literate. Don't do what one father did. After having caught his young son in a chat room exchanging pirated software, he later bought him a laptop and now provides no monitoring.

Don't Give Up—There's Hope!

Invaded by TV violence, barraged by the violent film images of the big screen, deafened by the sounds of violence, desensitized by the cyber-images of killing on video and computer games, addicted by the pornography and violence on the Internet—our culture in many ways stands in stark contrast to the kind of kingdom in which our teens need to live. Yet while we are in the world, we are not in darkness. Our teens can dwell in the kingdom of light and be light in the world. Encourage and warn them with the ancient biblical words of wisdom:

My child, if sinners entice you, turn your back on them! They may say, "Come and join us. Let's hide and kill someone! Let's ambush the innocent! Let's swallow them alive as the grave swallows its victims. Though they are in the prime of life, they will go down into the pit of death. And the loot we'll get! We'll fill our houses with all kinds of things! Come on, throw in your lot with us; we'll split our loot with you."

Don't go along with them, my child! Stay far away from their paths. They rush to commit crimes. They hurry to commit murder. When a bird sees a trap being set, it stays away. But not these people! They set an ambush for themselves; they booby-trap their own lives! Such is the fate of all who are greedy for gain. It ends up robbing them of life.

—PROVERBS 1:10–19

> *While we are in the world, we are not in darkness. Our teens can dwell in the kingdom of light and be light in the world.*

Eerily fulfilling these solemn warnings from the past, the recent shootings and high school acts of violence paint a grisly picture of what happens in a culture that worships surreal images that tragically become real life. But there is hope for those who heed these warnings and avoid such violence—both real and imagined.

> Trust in the LORD with all your heart; do not depend on your own understanding. Seek his will in all you do, and he will direct your paths. Don't be impressed with your own wisdom. Instead, fear the LORD and turn your back on evil. Then you will gain renewed health and vitality
> —PROVERBS 3:5–8

Lord of love, let this family be a sanctuary of peace for all who are weary of the fighting, troubled by the images of violence, saddened by the struggles of person against person. Be to us the selfsame Lord who said, "Peace, be still!"

Only eyes washed by tears can see clearly.

—Louis L. Mann

There is nothing to compare with the impact and profound shock of sudden and unexpected death. The assault is a jolt to the system. After a sudden death the period of shock and disbelief is long lasting. Those who have suffered the sudden death of a loved one will experience a long period of numbness and denial.[1]

Emotional Pain:
Dealing With Death

Dustin Scholle, a junior at Marengo Community High School, wrote: "You ask the question, Why do kids walk into a school and open fire on fellow classmates? It is because they have to feel love before they can give love. I am sorry for what happened, it cannot be stopped now. But it can be stopped in other places. I want to write this poem just for you."

I feel your pain
    on this day of sorrow.
I am sorry for what happened
    even though I don't know how.
My heart cries out to you
    with a big bellow
It is so loud I can't
    even swallow.
My brain is confused
    I can't figure out what to say.
All I know is I feel your pain.[2]

Dustin's a nice kid, like most teenagers you and I know. And he eloquently expresses the pain we all feel and our deep sadness for the families and friends who lost their loved ones through the tragic events at Littleton and in other towns. I, along with countless others across the world, are praying for you all.

Christians do not see death as final. Christ defeated death so that eternally we will never die.

Grief is a very real part of the Bible—David grieved over losing his son and his baby not yet born; Jacob grieved over the reported death of his son Joseph; Jeremiah grieved at the death of King Josiah; and the two sisters, Mary and Martha, grieved over the death of their brother, Lazarus. Yet the promise God gives us is that when confronted with death, His presence will be with us (Ps. 23). He is acquainted with our grief and will strengthen us (Isa. 53).

Of course, this is not to say that a Christian's emotional pain is less than an unbeliever's. It's just that Christians do not see death as final. Christ defeated death so that eternally we will never die. What an act of compassion from a loving God—sending His Son to die a terrible and cruel death so that we may live. And because of God's sacrifice, we will meet our loved ones again in eternity.

Even so, Jesus grieved. He wept with the sisters over the death of their brother. He grieved in the Garden of Gethsemane the night He was betrayed. And He preached, "Blessed are those who mourn, for they shall be comforted" (Matt. 5:4, NIV). Grieving is necessary if we are to cope with death.

Understanding Normal Grieving

Most people view the death of a child as one of life's greatest tragedies and challenges. Children are not supposed to die before their parents; it's out of sequence. Children are our most important emotional focus in a family. They are extensions of us, representing our hopes, dreams and unfulfilled expectations. We want to give our children all that we can. We love and esteem them, and we can't imagine our lives without them. Nothing can be as painful as losing a child, an event made even more horrible by the aspect of *sudden* death.

The sudden death of a child brings on intense and prolonged emotional pain. Adjusting to a child's death is more difficult than any other family life-cycle transition. We expect to help our children grow and to launch them into the world. When they abruptly die, that launching never occurs, the family life cycle is interrupted, and our dreams come crashing down.

All members of the family are shaken and affected by the tragedy. And with sudden death, there is no anticipated grieving. Siblings are frightened, feeling lost and confused, and marriages can come under tremendous strain. Sudden death raises apprehension about the future, brings on a sense of insecurity and is hard to grasp because of the overwhelming pain. Families who experience the sudden death of a child commonly ask several questions:

Did this really happen?

It will take time for the full impact of the loss to register with families. The initial reaction is unbelief, shock or numbness.

Could I have done something more—or differently?

"If only . . . " It's normal to rehearse various scenarios in our minds as to how we could have prevented the death. I remember my own brother's tragic death: "If only we'd brought Gary home for his brother's wedding, he wouldn't have been on that plane that crashed. If only he had let someone else go in his place. If only the plane had been delayed." It's easy to imagine the cruel cycle of tormenting questions raised by the families in Colorado: "*If only* my child had been sick that day. *If only* he got delayed going to lunch. *If only* she was in a different part of the building." While it is normal to have these thoughts, you cannot dwell on them and make yourself crazy. None of these fantasies can become reality now.

Am I worthy of living?

This thought is common. "What did I do to deserve to live?" I'll say more about this in the following section on survivor's guilt.

Who can I blame?

When we experience anything out of our control, we want to blame someone or something as a way to make sense of it. At the time of my brother's death, people blamed the airlines, terrorists, the Army and anyone else they could think of. We were encouraged to sue. As Christians we must be cautious with our initial responses and submit later responses to prayer before making decisions. In the heat of the moment, we usually don't make good choices. We often react only to the pain we feel inside.

Why do I have to deal with all these medical and legal authorities?

At the time of a sudden death, no one wants to deal with questions from police, coroners, doctors, investigators and other officials. We feel they are invading our private moments of grief, and they are. Yet sometimes these intrusive questions are vital to obtaining needed information. We also feel a sense of morbidity when we deal with funeral directors, the county coroner and others trying to make death arrangements. These people are accustomed to murder and death. Sometimes they appear insensitive and uncaring.

I remember when my friend George was electrocuted while trimming tree branches one Saturday morning. We were at the house of his widow trying to be a source of comfort to her and her three small children. The telephone rang incessantly with people asking questions like, "Can you see the body now?" "Was he an organ donor?" "What funeral home are you using?" It felt like an onslaught, and I wanted to shield her from these necessary but painful interruptions. Be sensitive to these things if you are a friend of the grieving. Help out by taking as many of those phone calls as possible.

Why can't I talk to him or her one more time?

Obviously, you can't prepare for sudden death because you don't know it is coming. The last thing said may have been pleasant and loving. Maybe you were able to give a last hug, smile at your child or tell her you loved her. Maybe you had an argument, were hurried that morning, didn't speak or had to discipline.

It's best to accept the fact that you may not have been able to resolve every problem you and your loved one experienced.

It's best to accept the fact that you may not have been able to resolve every problem you and your loved one experienced. If you can't accept this without excessive guilt, you may develop psychological or physical symptoms. Regrets and unfinished business are normal when sudden death occurs. Don't dwell on them. It serves no purpose.

God, why?

It's OK to ask this, and you will, many times. There is no easy answer. You may never know. I still don't know why my brother was killed more than twenty-five years ago. I no longer ask, because it's not so important anymore. I hold on to the promise that God works all circumstances together for my good. Maybe that's one reason I wrote this book.

Recognizing the Variety of Grief Responses

Although we tend to believe grief passes through consecutive stages, it doesn't. Grieving is a process in which a number of emotions and behaviors are revisited several times. There is no right order, and people tend to go back and forth with varying feelings. Grief is an automatic process in which a period of denial helps buy time to process the trauma.

Ways We Respond to Grief

We respond with . . . numbness, shock, denial, intense sorrow, pain, anger, confusion, loneliness, emptiness, depression, guilt, fear, abandonment, isolation, physical symptoms, irritability, fantasy, restlessness, disorganization, hopelessness and fear.

Grief is a time of stress that taxes the immune system, making the body more susceptible to illness. During grief, try to get good nutrition and plenty of rest. Physical symptoms can include headaches, fatigue, appetite loss, dizziness, heart palpitations, numbness, irritability and insomnia. The overall feeling is one of body exhaustion caused by the intensity of emotions. Other important things to keep in mind are:

1. There is no specific time limit to grieve.

Eventually, you will accept the loss and gradually adjust. There will always be a void; the loss is permanent. Time helps, but the pain never totally goes away. Remind yourself that suffering is part of life and can be used for growth. In my experience with patients, it usually takes about two years to move through the heavy grieving. The actual length of time, though, depends on a number of factors, including:

How the death occurred.

Sudden and unexpected death is more difficult to cope with than death by natural causes. And it's more difficult to cope with a violent death. Lack of information about the specifics of a death can prolong grief. My heart went out to the Littleton parents waiting to learn who was missing, who had died and when they could retrieve the bodies of their sons and daughters. Those hours were traumatic.

The history of previous losses.

Prior losses, particularly those that remain unresolved, intensify the current loss. I remember that when I miscarried my first pregnancy, the grief rolled over me like a tide. Miscarriage is a painful loss and should not be minimized in any way. But at the time of the miscarriage, I was acutely aware of other losses in my life. The death of my brother when I was seventeen hit me again. The miscarriage not only forced me to deal with current grief related to the situation, but it also forced me to deal with left-over business from the death of my brother. Once again, I faced uncertainty and fear, felt alone and abandoned and had to revisit these issues in prayer.

The timing in the life cycle.

Coping with death at any time of life is painful. As we move through the life cycle, we come to a point in our development in which we have to face our own mortality. For most people this happens when grandparents or great-grandparents die. Coping with the death of an elderly person, while painful, is still expected as part of the ebb and flow of life. Again, I am not minimizing the death of anyone who has lost a loved one. The point is that when death occurs at a time in the life cycle that is thoroughly unexpected, coping is more diffi-

Sudden and unexpected death is more difficult to cope with than death by natural causes.

cult. Part of the struggle for the families of murder victims is that they are unprepared for the timing of the deaths of their children. We know it's not supposed to happen this soon.

2. Grief needs to be shared.

Norman Paul, a well-known family therapist who writes about loss, speaks to the importance of sharing our grief. He reflects that the healing, in part, is in telling our story. My personal experiences, combined with the experiences of people I treat, validate this. I highly recommend that the entire family sit down and recount the events of the death and talk about their responses. This will be easier for some than for others. But it is necessary. I can't emphasize enough the healing that takes place when each family member recalls his or her place in the unfolding of events. It not only helps to tell the story out loud, but it also heightens the awareness of all family members to the pain and suffering of the others. There is comfort in knowing you are not alone.

3. It's best to keep communication open.

As noted above, families must periodically talk about what happened. If you don't, you risk developing symptoms later. Don't keep your emotions pent up in an effort to be "strong." Again, drawing from my brother's death, it was helpful to see both parents cry and show pain. My mother, like most women, reacted immediately by crying and verbalizing her pain. My father's release of emotions came later, but they came.

I remember lying in bed one night shortly after Gary was killed and thinking, *This is too much for anyone to bear.* Above me, I could hear my father crying out to God, pounding the floor and weeping in anguish. Although his response was intense, it helped me. It gave me permission to release more emotion and not feel I had to be strong for anyone.

4. Get support—plenty of it.

During a time of tragedy, families do better when they can support one another. Watch your irritability, and don't blame those around you or bring up issues from the past. Don't isolate yourself from family members. They need you, and you need them. Your physical presence is especially reassuring to children. It's also okay to tell people when you need to be alone.

Furthermore, some people find it helpful to join a grief support group, especially one organized around similar types of death: for example, sudden death, chronic illness, elderly parents and death of a spouse.

The idea is to learn to let other people help you. If someone offers to bring a meal, let them. If someone wants to clean your house, thank them. If someone wants to answer the telephone and screen calls, say yes. This is a time to accept the support of others. There will be times in the future for you to do the same.

5. Previous family stress plays a role.

Grief may be affected by the level of family stress prior to the death. All families experience stress, some more than others. If family stress was high before the death occurred, coping may be more difficult. If after the death new family stress occurs, then coping becomes even more difficult. Some examples of family stress are the recent death of a parent, a separation, a divorce, financial struggles, extreme work pressures, a drug or alcohol problem in the family, abuse and lack of support.

6. The level of your prior emotional connection is important.

The more significant the child was to the overall

functioning of the family, the more you will notice the loss of this child in everyday life. The more dependent other family members were on the teen, the more the loss will be felt. For example, if the child shot was a primary babysitter for a working parent, the parent faces immediate grief—and the additional stress of finding child care.

Not only does the nuclear family grieve, but the relatives who may live at a distance will also grieve. Such is the reality for Danny Rohrbough's grandfather, Claude. Since he was three, Danny helped his grandfather harvest wheat every July on the family's Kansas farm. He would travel from Littleton to his grandparents' house for the summer ritual. Last year, Danny even got to drive the diesel combine that harvested the wheat. Now his absence will create a huge void in his grandparents' lives. When asked about the loss of his grandson, Danny's grandfather reportedly took an eternity to respond and finally said, "We'll miss his help. We'll have to find a way to do it without him." You just know that driving a combine and harvesting wheat was only the surface of a deep, lasting emotional connection between a grandson and grandfather.

During a time of tragedy, families do better when they can support one another.

7. Rituals are helpful in remembering the death.

In Littleton, we saw teens showering flowers on the trucks and parked cars of those who were killed. Memorial services were held. Symbolic acts of good-bye were numerous.

Rituals should be personal and encouraged. Tell children and teens about death and include them in the mourning process. I believe we should give children the opportunity to attend the funeral, view the body (if that is part of your tradition) and say good-bye. Most children want to go to the funeral when given the opportunity. But you know your child best, and you need to decide what will help him or her the most. Make the decision based on the child's best interest and not on your own discomfort with issues surrounding death.

8. It's important to talk about the person who died.

It helps to tell stories and to reminisce. Everyone is adjusting to the loss of the teen. Acting as though it didn't happen won't help. On the other hand, don't talk about the deceased all the time. Try to keep a balance. If you over-focus, you set up the possibility for feelings of resentment among remaining family members. In this regard, be careful not to idealize the person who died. Over time, talk about his or her strengths and weaknesses.

9. Keep busy and active in your church.

After the initial period of grieving, begin to resume

as many of your normal activities as possible. This helps you manage your thoughts and emotions. Do what you can. Avoid extremes. Don't be rushed into doing things too soon nor preoccupied with activity that may prevent your feelings from surfacing.

Your church can give you spiritual support and remind you of God's presence and concern. Times of corporate worship are meaningful moments for sharing grief as a family.

10. Finally, you will have to come to terms with forgiveness.

We have no choice but to forgive—not because the killers deserve it, not because it's easy or natural to do, but because Jesus commanded it. Some may also have to face the prospect of forgiving God. Others may face forgiving themselves.

Jesus taught, "If you forgive those who sin against you, your heavenly Father will forgive you. But if you refuse to forgive others, your Father will not forgive your sins" (Matt. 6:14–15). In the same way that He forgives us though we are undeserving, we need to extend forgiveness to others, even those who have deeply hurt us and taken our loved ones. Forgiveness is a choice of the will; the emotions follow. If we do not forgive, we leave ourselves open to bitterness and block our intimacy with God.

It's clear to me that while Christians understand that a funeral is a celebration and a time to rejoice in Christ's victory over death, we also need to grieve. *Genuine joy is never a denial of normal grief.* It is one of God's mysterious gifts to His followers. It may feel as though God has abandoned you when you walk the road of sorrow. But He hasn't. It's okay to tell Him how upset you are and share your deepest feelings with Him. He created all of you, including your emotions.

Grieving comes and goes in intensity. Some days you feel you are doing well, and other days are just hard to get through. At times, you will be surprised at how the most insignificant thing can bring on an outpouring of grief. At other times, you will be amazed at your strength. Through it all, you'll discover that His grace is sufficient to meet all your needs. Hear Jesus say to you, "My grace is sufficient for thee: for my strength is made perfect in weakness" (2 Cor. 12:9, KJV). His strong arms surround you with comfort and love.

> *We have no choice but to forgive—not because the killers deserve it, not because it's easy or natural to do, but because Jesus commanded it.*

> The eternal God is your refuge, and his everlasting arms are under you.
>
> DEUTERONOMY 22:27

Severe Signs of Grief

It's important to watch for more severe signs of grief that may create deeper psychological problems, such as:

- Substance abuse

- Chronic psychosomatic complaints

- Excessive guilt

- Wanting to die and join the person who died

- Morbid preoccupation with worthlessness

- Inability to get back into a routine after a significant period of time

- Overly intense reactions when the deceased is mentioned

- Isolation from normal relationships

- Feelings of intense hostility or irritability

If your physical symptoms of grief—or any of the problems above—linger for more than two months and are interfering with your functioning, you may need to talk to a grief counselor. This time frame is only a reference. You will know if you are getting stuck in your grief. If so, help is available.

Helping the Survivors Heal

Many have asked, "What about those who were there at Columbine High School during the shootings and survived?" Here is one description of an injured survivor at the scene:

Richard Castaldo is paralyzed from the shoulders down. He was eating lunch outside when he was cut down where he sat by a burst of semiautomatic weapons fire. Five bullets ripped through his chest and back, fragmenting two vertebrae between his shoulder blades. "Everything north of that works," said trauma surgeon William Pfeifer. Castaldo asked his dad who was killed at Columbine. He cried as the names of classmates were recited. He couldn't lift his hands to wipe his tears.[3]

Like Richard Castaldo, some of the students were physically wounded, and others were traumatized psychologically. How will Evan Todd, a fifteen-year-old sophomore, who reportedly was hiding behind the main library desk during the mayhem, go back to normal life after having a shooter point a gun to his head and ask why he should live?

Reports say Aaron Cohn, fifteen, was studying in the library when he saw a pipe-bomb come through the window. Then the shooters emerged shouting, "All the jocks stand up. We are going to kill you."[4] The girl next to him jumped in front of Aaron in order to hide his athletic T-shirt. The gunman approached her, put a gun to her head and asked if she wanted to die. She and Aaron were spared, but the impact of that trauma will be with them for a long time.

Many, many others survived the terror physically, but they were eyewitnesses to the horror—blood-soaked clothing, bodies on the ground, teens running for their lives, SWAT teams and police everywhere. They experienced great trauma.

Coping With Sudden Death

Allow yourself to grieve. Give vent to your intense emotions. This sudden death has allowed you no opportunity to prepare yourself; therefore, you will be going through all the stages of grieving after the death. It is better to express—rather than suppress—these feelings.

Grief is not terminal. God transforms our sorrow into joy as He heals our sadness.

Tears give release to sorrow.

Though you feel God has deserted you, the Bible assures you that God has promised the Holy Spirit as your Comforter (Heb. 13:5; John 14:16). God is as saddened as you are right now.

Your body's grief reaction is normal. You may experience disturbing physical symptoms.

Follow what feels right for you. Don't let others dissuade you from doing what is meaningful for you.

Tell friends and relatives how you want to be treated. At times, say, "I want to be alone," if that is your wish.

Share your troublesome thoughts and feelings with an understanding, nurturing friend. Giving vent to feelings with a friend who can listen with acceptance helps dispel the feelings' intensity.

Join a support group or grief recovery program. Call your local hospital or ask your pastor if such groups exist in your community. Seek counseling with a pastor or psychologist if you feel continually overwhelmed.

Keep busy, but not to the point that you stop the grieving process. Take time to mourn and let go.

Give meaning to your life through helping others. Try to do things that you feel are worthwhile so you can have good thoughts and feelings about yourself.

Keep active in a church where Christian friends will continue to show support.

Recognize there will always be a void. The pain will lessen as time and life go on, but you may always feel your loved one's absence and have the feeling your family is incomplete.

Recognize that suffering engenders growth. On your own timetable, and with God's help, you will survive and eventually heal.

Use Scriptures like these during your quiet times: Deuteronomy 33:27; Psalms 46:1–2; 91:14–15; Isaiah 54:1–7; John 14:1–7, 15–21.[7]

Helping Those Who Grieve

The most important thing anyone can do to help the individual or family grieving the loss of a loved one is to pray with and for that person or family—assuring them of God's never-failing love and mercy and comfort. Then use the following guidelines to help you extend God's love in a tangible way to that family.

- At the time of the crisis, stay with the family.

- Don't offer platitudes; they aren't helpful and feel insincere to the griever.

- Use the word *death*; don't skirt around it.

- Respect the grieving family's timing on grieving; don't try to force emotions that aren't there yet.

- Remain calm and comforting.

- Talk about the death if they ask you to.

- Ask if there is anyone who needs to be called and offer to do it.

- Ask relatives and friends what needs to be done around the house and do it. Don't ask the person who is grieving.

- You don't need to offer a lot of words. Just be there.

- Don't say, "This is God's will."

- This is not the time to discuss your personal stories.

- Give them space when they need it; be available when they need you.

- Don't say, "But you have other children."

- Affirm their feelings.

- Remember the significant dates from the deceased person's life with a card, note, phone call or visit to the surviving family.

Trama Disorders

When people are traumatized, they may react with Acute Stress Disorder or Post-Traumatic Stress Disorder. *Acute Stress Disorder* is a psychological condition that occurs after a person has witnessed a traumatic event like the one at Columbine. The teens there were threatened with death, saw others die or were hurt or injured. Some witnessed others being hurt and injured. When the reaction to such trauma is fear, helplessness or horror, survivors can experience some of the following feelings over a four-week period. They may:

- Feel numb, detached or emotionally unresponsive.

- Feel as if they are in a daze.

- Feel as if they are in a dream.

- Feel detached from one's body.

- Have difficulty recollecting important aspects of the trauma.

The trauma replays itself in one of these ways: recurrent images, thoughts, dreams, illusions, flashback episodes, sense of reliving the experience, or distress when exposed to reminders of the event. There is a desire to avoid things that recall the trauma, with symptoms of anxiety such as irritability, sleep difficulties, etc. Functioning is impaired. [5]

Acute Stress Disorder usually begins and ends within a month's time frame. If the symptoms persist, they become *Post-Traumatic Stress Disorder* (PTSD). Symptoms usually begin within three months of the trauma, but they can be delayed as well. The chances of developing the disorder relate to the severity, duration and proximity of the exposure to the trauma. This means that those who had guns pointed at their heads and saw other kids shot next to them are more at risk. Other factors, such as family history, supports and faith, may also relate to risk.

With Christ, we can supernaturally rise above fear and anxiety.

This disorder can develop when someone is a witness to death, physical harm or the threat of death, and he responds to the trauma with fear, helplessness or horror. The traumatic event is *re-experienced* in one or more of these ways:

- Has intrusive, recurrent and distressing recollections

- Has recurrent and distressing dreams

- Feels as if the trauma is recurring

- Has psychological distress with anything resembling the event

- Has physical distress at things that resemble the trauma

Overall, there is a numbing and difficulty with sleep, anger, concentration, hypervigilence and being startled.[6]

Emotional Pain: Dealing With Death

"Survivor's guilt" is also a common response to traumatic death. Siblings who survive often feel guilty for not dying also. They may experience guilt, confusion, isolation and fear. They may wonder if they will die next and may develop behavioral problems, physical complaints, depression and, at times, feelings of suicide. Siblings may feel "haunted by the dead" and become phobic. Other fears and anxieties may begin to surface, such as not wanting to leave home or needing to stay close to parents for comfort.

Parents' responses to teens who survive trauma are critical. They need to take seriously the complaints and anxieties their kids may feel. They should ask the teens how they feel about surviving when some of their friends did not.

Fear and anxiety are raised to a new level for survivors. Will they be hurt again? Can they stop thinking about the trauma? In the natural, fear is a primary response. With Christ, we can supernaturally rise above fear and anxiety. This doesn't mean we deny the reality of circumstances or that trauma doesn't affect us. It means we have added strength to deal with the situation because of Christ in us. (See 1 John 4:4 and Matthew 6:25, 33–35.) Jesus said, "Be anxious about nothing." How is this possible, given such horrific events? It's only possible when we think on Him, meditating on what He's done through the cross and what He promises to do—give us rest and a peace that passes understanding.

Transformed Grief

Yes, there are tribulations in this world, and evil has its day. We aren't always removed from evil circumstances. However, God always knows what we suffer and He can work it for our good. Remember that grief is not terminal. God transforms our sorrow into joy as He heals our sadness. He says:

> I will turn their mourning into gladness; I will give them comfort and joy instead of sorrow.
> —JEREMIAH 31:13, NIV

For Those of Us Who Watched . . .

Because of pervasive media coverage, we are all witnesses to the traumas of school shootings. We don't know what to say, how to share the pain or how to tell the families involved that we care. Listen to how some of the onlookers have expressed themselves:

> I was just completely overwhelmed . . . I have ideas about how to change the world. When I see kids killing kids—I just wasn't connected until August when I became a teacher.
> —A teacher at Marengo High School[8]

> Last night I had a dream and awoke with fear. Unfortunately, it was not a dream; instead, it was reality. Reality for every student, because now we have to live in fear. In fear of each

other, of violence, in fear of living in the world that we do.

—Sarah Draper, freshman [9]

As I watched the events at Columbine High School unfold in my own living room, I was shocked, horrified, disarmed, anxious, prayerful and much more. I could hardly take the intensity of my emotions—and I was only a distant bystander. Imagine, then, what it must have been like for the families and teens who lived out the drama.

Consider the story of Rachel Scott. Her mother and stepfather, Larry and Beth Nimmo, appeared on TBN's *Praise the Lord* on Wednesday, May 5 and recounted the terrible events that led to her murder because she loved Jesus.

I'm not going to hide the light that God has put in me. If I have to sacrifice everything, I will take it.

First the shooters shot her in the leg, then they ran her down and finally they held a gun to her face and cocked the hammer back.

"Do you believe in God?" they asked.

"Yes."

"Then go to be with Him."

They shot her in the temple, killing her.

Rachel had been ostracized for her faith in Christ and had spent many lonely hours at school. One year to the day before she was killed, April 20, 1998, she wrote in her journal:

> But you know what, it's all worth it to me. I'm not going to apologize for speaking the name, "Jesus." I'm not going to justify my faith to them. I'm not going to hide the light that God has put in me. If I have to sacrifice everything, I will take it. If my friends have to be my enemies for me to be with my best friend, Jesus, then that's fine with me.

At the school, Rachel's car, a red Acura Legend, was turned into a memorial by the folks who knew her and what she stood for. There was a cross laid next to the car, and on the vertical beam were the words, "Fear not." On the horizontal beam: "For God is already there."

Amazingly, now even the secular press is reporting about this kind of bold faith among believing kids, and they are being influenced by it. The Nimmos reported that one of the reporters came to their son Craig (also a hero) after an interview and said, "Whatever you've got, I want."

In Rachel's eulogy, her pastor spoke of how Rachel bore the torch of truth, compassion, love and the Good News of Jesus Christ. The pastor's challenge was this: "The torch has fallen from Rachel's hand—who will pick it up again?" On the program they reported that many teens stood up in the funeral and are responding to the challenge. Apparently teens all over are responding with renewed zeal and radical faith in Christ.

Emotional Pain: Dealing With Death

Larry Nimmo reported that one of the first thoughts in his mind when he learned of Rachel's death was the scripture, "He will crush your head, and you will strike his heel" (Gen. 3:15). What Satan meant for evil to derail God's plan and God's people, God is overruling for good. For through this, souls are being saved and young people are spreading the fire of the gospel.

The Nimmos have been powerfully affected with grief and also inspired in hope. We all have been affected in some way. We all began to question the safety of our world. We all hugged our kids a little harder that week, and we all wanted to make sense of something so senseless. Some looked for answers in the steady stream of reports. Some relived their own personal pain. Others didn't want to think about it. Still others talked about Columbine at work, school and play, secretly and openly wondering: *Could it happen here?*

When bad things happen, we want to make sense of them. We want to feel in control, and we wish we could stop the evil. Often we can't. Yet this we know: Evil will finally be defeated when Jesus returns. We can hold on to the promises, here and hereafter, until that day.

For no matter how many promises God has made, they are "Yes" in Christ. And so through him the "Amen" is spoken to the glory of God.

—2 CORINTHIANS 1:20, NIV

141

Part Three:
The Hope

I believe that unarmed truth and unconditional love will have the final word in reality. This is why right temporarily defeated is stronger than evil triumphant.

— Dr. Martin Luther King, Jr. [1]

And now I am no more in the world, but these are in the world, and I come to thee. Holy Father, keep through thine own name those whom thou hast given me, that they may be one, as we are. While I was with them in the world, I kept them in thy name: those that thou gavest me I have kept, and none of them is lost, but the son of perdition; that the scripture might be fulfilled. And now come I to thee; and these things I speak in the world, that they might have my joy fulfilled in themselves. I have given them thy word; and the world hath hated them, because they are not of the world, even as I am not of the world. I pray not that thou shouldest take them out of the world, but that thou shouldest keep them from the evil. They are not of the world, even as I am not of the world.

—JOHN 17:11–16, KJV

A Faith Perspective on School Violence

At Columbine High School, thirteen people were killed by the shooters. According to some reports, eight of those killed were Christians. In particular, we have accounts that one died a martyr—Cassie Bernall.

> It was a test all of us would hope to pass, but none of us really wants to take. A masked gunman points his weapon at a Christian and asks, "Do you believe in God?" She knows that if she says "yes," she'll pay with her life. But unfaithfulness to her Lord is unthinkable. So, with what would be her last words, she calmly answers, "Yes, I believe in God."[2]

In this commentary, Chuck Colson, who wrote these words, proceeded to cite a *Washington Post* report that the shooters did not randomly choose their victims but acted out of a "kaleidoscope of ugly prejudices."

America's litany of recent high school shootings

reminds us once again that no matter how safe and normal the world appears to be—life is fragile; hate, prejudice and persecution do exist; suffering is a reality; and trusting Christ is our only security.

So how do we go on, knowing that a precious loved one's life could be extinguished at any moment like a sudden burst of wind robbing a candle of its light? Classmate Mickie Cain told Larry King on CNN:

> She [Cassie] completely stood up for God. When the killers asked her if there was anyone who had faith in Christ, she spoke up, and they shot her for it.

Cassie's friend, Craig Moon, called her a "light for Christ."

There is a message for all of us in her faithful witness. She was a light in the darkness, fulfilling what Jesus called us to be:

> You are the light of the world—like a city on a mountain, glowing in the night for all to see. Don't hide your light under a basket! Instead, put it on a stand and let it shine for all. In the same way, let your good deeds shine out for all to see, so that everyone will praise your heavenly Father.
>
> —MATTHEW 5:14–16

In pointing us to Christ, Cassie's witness directs us to the only One who gives us hope in the midst of kids killing kids. In Christ, we can find the comfort and the strength to address these tragedies without fear. We fear no evil because God has given us love, power and a sound mind (2 Tim. 1:7).

These are great and wonderful promises. But let's take a moment to remember that some of the things we may assume God has said, He has *not* said. That is, in God's Word, we can uncover both what God has *not* promised us in times like these and what He *has* promised.

God DIDN'T Promise . . .

God is all-wise and all-loving in every way. Therefore we can assume that the things He does not promise will add to His glory and our spiritual growth. Consider:

God didn't promise an escape from all suffering.

While Jesus prayed that the Father would keep us from evil, He did remind us that in the world we would have great difficulties: "I have told you all

So, with what would be her last words, Cassie calmly answers, "Yes, I believe in God."

this so that you may have peace in me. Here on earth you will have many trials and sorrows. But take heart, because I have overcome the world" (John 16:33).

Yes, in this world, those who love Christ like Cassie Bernall will face fierce and heartless attacks. Again, Jesus taught us:

God blesses those who are persecuted because they live for God, for the Kingdom of Heaven is theirs. God blesses you when you are mocked and persecuted and lied about because you are my followers. Be happy about it! Be very glad! For a great reward awaits you in heaven. And remember, the ancient prophets were persecuted, too.

—MATTHEW 5:10–12

Of course, we never rejoice when someone is tragically killed. But we do rejoice that a believer's death is not meaningless or in vain. We are happy that the one we loved has reaped the reward of eternal life, but we are saddened at our painful loss. The reality of living in a fallen, sinful world is that evil exists and the righteous along with the unrighteous will suffer. Again Jesus instructs us, "And ye shall be hated of all men for my name's sake: but he that endureth to the end shall be saved" (Matt. 10:22, KJV).

Cassie endured to the end. Her courageous faith is a lighthouse for us to follow in a storm-tossed world. She reminds me of the great saints of the church who set the example of putting everything else in the background of their lives in order to pursue the Lord wholeheartedly. Listen to one of them:

My God, I choose the whole lot. No point in becoming a saint by halves. I'm not afraid of suffering for your sake; the only thing I'm afraid of is clinging to my own will. Take it. I want the whole lot, everything whatsoever that is your will for me.

—THERESE OF LISIEUX

In a similar vein, centuries before these shootings, the apostle Paul wrote that life is defined not by suffering and death, but by living for Christ:

> According to my earnest expectation and my hope, that in nothing I shall be ashamed, but that with all boldness, as always, so now also Christ shall be magnified in my body, whether it be by life, or by death. For to me to live is Christ, and to die is gain.
>
> —PHILIPPIANS 1:20–21, KJV

Christ Himself was one who was acquainted with grief, pain and suffering. As we trust Him, we too will participate in His suffering:

> Yes, everything else is worthless when compared with the priceless gain of knowing Christ Jesus my Lord. I have discarded everything else, counting it all as garbage, so that I may have Christ and become one with him. I no longer count on my own goodness or my ability to obey God's law, but I trust Christ to save me. For God's way of making us right with himself depends on faith. As a result, I can really know Christ and experience the mighty power that raised him from the dead. I can learn what it means to suffer with him, sharing in his death, so that, somehow, I can experience the resurrection from the dead!
>
> —PHILIPPIANS 3:8–11

God didn't promise we would understand everything.

Understanding why it all happened is beyond human reason. We can look at all the puzzle pieces and still come up with some missing. Yes, the culture, families, school cliques, Internet bomb information, violent video games, brutal music lyrics, psychic pain and many other factors had varying degrees of impact on the lives of the shooters. Yet, news reports also tell just how normal the lives of these teens were, even up to a few days before the Littleton shootings.[3] As the apostle Paul writes, "For now we see through a glass, darkly; but then face to face" (1 Cor. 13:12, KJV).

On May 2, 1999, a commentator on *CNN's Headline News* filed a report from Littleton. He reported how the police, in sifting through all the evidence, had determined what had happened and who was responsible for the killing. But the reporter lamented, "The one unanswered question is: Why?"

That is the question that keeps haunting us all, the mystery that will keep demanding explanation. Yet only partial answers exist for such a tragedy. We live in an evil world, and darkness lurks in the hidden recesses of human hearts: "The human heart is most deceitful and desperately wicked. Who really knows how bad it is?" (Jer. 17:9). We must also acknowledge that life is filled with mystery. When Job suffered the loss of all his children after hedging them about with prayer, and lost his possessions and health, he cried out to God for answers. The Lord's mystery-filled response was:

Then the LORD answered Job from the whirlwind: "Who is this that questions my wisdom with such ignorant words? Brace yourself, because I have some questions for you, and you must answer them.

"Where were you when I laid the foundations of the earth? Tell me, if you know so much. Do you know how its dimensions were determined and who did the surveying? What supports its foundations, and who laid its cornerstone as the morning stars sang together and all the angels shouted for joy?

"Who defined the boundaries of the sea as it burst from the womb, and as I clothed it with clouds and thick darkness? For I locked it behind barred gates, limiting its shores. I said, 'Thus far and no farther will you come. Here your proud waves must stop!'

"Have you ever commanded the morning to appear and caused the dawn to rise in the east? Have you ever told the daylight to spread to the ends of the earth, to bring an end to the night's wickedness? For the features of the earth take shape as the light approaches, and the dawn is robed in red. The light disturbs the haunts of the wicked, and it stops the arm that is raised in violence.

"Have you explored the springs from which the seas come? Have you walked about and explored their depths? Do you know where the gates of death are located? Have you seen the gates of utter gloom? Do you realize the extent of the earth? Tell me about it if you know!"

—JOB 38:1–18

Ultimately, the answers to all the "whys" of these tragic killings will remain hidden until we meet Jesus face to face. But for now, let's move on to some good news.

God DID Promise . . .

God has certainly not left us without great and precious promises. We can boldly rely upon the decrees of our God, which never fail and which last forever. We can and should expect to emerge victorious from all our struggles, here or there.

Ultimately, the answers to all the "whys" of these tragic killings will remain hidden until we meet Jesus face to face.

God did promise that He would never leave nor forsake us.

We have a personal God who takes us by the hand and walks close to us through every trial. In the cafeteria of Columbine High School, when Cassie and others faced death, God was there. He never abandons us. "Yea, though I walk through the valley of the shadow of death, I will fear no evil: for thou art with me; thy rod and thy staff they comfort me" (Ps. 23:4, KJV). We may never understand why Cassie and other innocent kids died. But we do know one undeniable truth: God never leaves us nor forsakes us. I believe His presence inspired Cassie's courageous faith in the face of death.

God's abiding presence strengthens and comforts us as we face life's harshest pain and deepest hurts. We are not alone. We are never abandoned: "Be strong and courageous! Do not be afraid of them! The LORD your God will go ahead of you. He will neither fail you nor forsake you" (Deut. 31:6).

We can face all that the world throws at us when we know that God is with us. We can walk by faith through pain and even death when we trust the One who has already been where we are going. Christ has gone before us to prepare the way:

> Don't be troubled. You trust God, now trust in me. There are many rooms in my Father's home, and I am going to prepare a place for you. If this were not so, I would tell you plainly. When everything is ready, I will come and get you, so that you will always be with me where I am. And you know where I am going and how to get there.
> —JOHN 14:1–4

So Jesus' promise becomes our confidence in walking through every valley and facing every trial: "And be sure of this: I am with you always, even to the end of the age" (Matt. 28:20).

God did promise to comfort and protect us.

Ultimately, we have nothing to fear from evil. Over three hundred times in Scripture God tells us to *fear not!* Knowing how timid and frightened sheep can be, God gave us the Good Shepherd—Jesus Christ. He reminds us, "The thief's purpose is to steal and kill and destroy. My purpose is to give life in all its fullness. I am the good shepherd. The good shepherd lays down his life for the sheep" (John 10:10–11). Our human tendency is to fear those who can physically harm us. But Jesus reassures us, "Don't be afraid of those who want to kill you. They can only kill your body; they cannot touch your soul. Fear only God, who can destroy both soul and body in hell" (Matt. 10:28).

God has not given us a spirit of fear, but He gives us love, power and a sound mind (2 Tim. 1:7). So we can release fear and hold fast to His strength and comfort. God's Word promises:

> He comforts us in all our troubles so that we can comfort others. When others are troubled, we will be able to give them the same comfort God has given us. You can be sure that the more we suffer for Christ, the more God will shower us with his comfort through Christ.
>
> —2 CORINTHIANS 1:4–5

God's protecting love shelters us; His perfect love expels all our fear (1 John 4:18). The psalmist's song gives foundation to our trust in the Lord:

> Those who live in the shelter of the Most High
> will find rest in the shadow of the Almighty.
> This I declare of the LORD:
> He alone is my refuge, my place of safety;
> he is my God, and I am trusting him.
>
> —PSALM 91:1–2

God did promise to work in all things for the good of those who love Him.

Can anything good come out of these tragic shootings? God didn't cause these tragedies. Kids decided to kill kids. Wrong choices were made. Evil plans were devised. And kids acted of their own free will to hurt others.

But again: Can anything good come out of it? We do know that the final word does not rest with the shooters, the reporters, the police, the media or the world. The final word resides in the Cassies of this world who bear the Light. We can make good plans and battle evil. The last word is not with lost boys killing others, but with children of light bringing life and hope to others. As that happens, good springs forth.

God is at work for good in all of this. His Word reveals, "And we know that in all things God works for the good of those who love him, who have been called according to his purpose" (Rom. 8:28, NIV). George MacDonald, a great writer of the last century, said it like this:

No words can express how much the world owes to sorrow. Most of the psalms were born in a wilderness. Most of the epistles were written in a prison. The greatest thoughts of the greatest thinkers have all passed through the fire. . . . Take comfort, afflicted Christian! When God is about to make preeminent use of a [person], He puts him in the fire.

God is at work in us to accomplish His good plans, in spite of an evil world.

> "For I know the plans I have for you," says the LORD. "They are plans for good and not for disaster, to give you a future and a hope. In those days when you pray, I will listen."
> —JEREMIAH 29:11–12

These shootings can become a wake-up call for us as Christian not to fear but to fight, not to withdraw but to engage the enemy and possess the land. God promises, "Then if my people who are called by my name will humble themselves and pray and seek my face and turn from their wicked ways, I will hear from heaven and will forgive their sins and heal their land" (2 Chron. 7:14.)

What Are We to Do—Spiritually?

It was reported that when a contractor in Littleton constructed fifteen crosses along a ridge overlooking Columbine High School, Brian Rohrbough, the father of one of the victims, removed the two crosses bearing the killers' names.[4] Makeshift crosses were quickly erected replacing the removed ones. That's what we are to do! We are to bring the cross of Christ into the world, replacing the darkness of hate, unforgiveness and revenge.

As Christians, we have spiritual work to do in the aftermath of these tragedies. That work is to be a witness in the world, bringing light so that all will glorify God.

Here is some of the spiritual work ahead of us. As followers of Jesus Christ, the light of the world, we are called to . . .

Pray and intercede.

Pray for the families of the victims and the killers. Pray that all will come to a saving knowledge of Jesus Christ. Pray that God will bring healing and reconciliation to the students, families and communities involved in all the places where kids have killed kids. Such prayers will not be offered in vain.

> God puts our prayers like rose-leaves between the leaves of His book of remembrance. And when the volume is opened at last, there shall be a precious fragrance springing from them.[5]

Forgive.

Jesus warns us that God cannot forgive us unless we forgive others. (See Matthew 6:14–15.) Forgiveness begins with everyone forgiving the kids who killed kids. And forgiveness goes even further. There must be reconciling forgiveness among cliques and reconciliation among races and genders. The hate that was experienced between races and teen cliques has to be replaced with God's healing love.

The final word resides in the Cassies of this world who bear the Light.

Engage in spiritual warfare.

It's time to put on the full armor of God and to fight—not against flesh and blood, but against the evil principalities and powers that have cancerously infected our schools, media, music, Internet, games and culture at large. As the apostle Paul writes in Ephesians 6, we are not battling against people, but . . .

> against the evil rulers and authorities of the unseen world, against those mighty powers of darkness who rule this world, and against wicked spirits in the heavenly realms. Use every piece of God's armor to resist the enemy in the time of evil, so that after the battle you will still be standing firm.
>
> —EPHESIANS 6:12–13

Take responsibility as parents.

Much of what can be learned from these tragedies tracks back to parenting. We are not laying the blame at the feet of any one person or group. But we are saying that these shootings are a wake-up call to all parents: Let us not be detached from the daily lives of our children. We have a responsibility to be lovingly "in their faces" daily. How? As living examples of Christ. As mentors, teachers and guides in the ways of the Lord. God commands you and me to:

> Love the LORD your God with all your heart, all your soul, and all your strength. And you must commit yourselves wholeheartedly to these commands I am giving you today. Repeat them again and again to

your children. Talk about them when you are at home and when you are away on a journey, when you are lying down and when you are getting up again. Tie them to your hands as a reminder, and wear them on your forehead. Write them on the doorposts of your house and on your gates.

—DEUTERONOMY 6:5–9

Reach out to the alienated.

Instead of shunning teens who espouse lifestyles of rebellion, suppose we were to reach out to them? Churches, youth groups, school Bible studies, Christian athletic organizations, Christian music groups and the whole Christian community must find ways to communicate the good news of God's love to kids at risk in our culture. Too much of what we have done condemns them. Instead, we can love them without endorsing their lifestyles. Jesus commands us to love our enemies and to pray for them. Love takes action and makes contact—builds relationships, finds needs and meets them, finds hurts and heals them.

Get involved.

Fear may cause some Christian parents to flee to private schools and abandon public ones. However, Jesus sent us into the world to be salt and light right where we are. Perhaps it's time to get even more involved in our public schools. It's time for Christians to lead the fight for prayer and for the unborn among our youth who are being baptized by a prayerless educational system and a culture that winks at murdering the innocent—even in the womb. Christians need to be more involved as teachers, administrators and school board members. Fearful retreat is not an option.

Build support and keep networking.

Christians can build support networks for kids and parents. We need to help one another in knowing what our kids are doing and what others—particularly those motivated by greed and evil—are doing to our kids. We need to tear down the fences around our home churches and become unified bodies in our communities. Then we'll be Christians working and praying together with one voice and one accord so that the world sees Him— not religious factions fighting one another.

Clearly, we cannot sit back and hope things will get better. Whatever your view of the end times may be, the signs are all around us that wickedness and lawlessness are increasing. Scripture warns:

> In the last days there will be very difficult times. For people will love only themselves and their money. They will be boastful and proud, scoffing at God, disobedient to their parents, and ungrateful. They will consider nothing sacred. They will be unloving and unforgiving; they will slander others and have no self-control; they will be cruel and have no interest in what is good. They will betray their friends, be reckless, be puffed up with pride, and love pleasure rather than God. They will act as if they are religious, but they will reject the power that could make them godly. You must stay away from people like that.
>
> —2 TIMOTHY 3:1–5

A Faith Perspective on School Violence

So, whatever it takes
I will be one who lives in the flesh
Newness of life of those who are
Alive from the dead.

—Cassie Bernall,
martyred at Columbine High School,
wrote this poem just two days before her death.

The Aftermath: The Most Important Thing Left to Do

I realize that in this book I have given you a lot to think about and to do. As we look at all this information, try to assimilate it and then ponder what to do, we may feel overwhelmed and inadequate. So we wonder:

Can we raise healthy children?

Can we protect them?

The call to us as parents and responsible adults is to equip ourselves and our children with the Word of God to face the challenges of life. We can't do this without being on our knees in continual intercession. We also need to hide the Word of God in our hearts so that when we're squeezed in times of crisis, what comes out of us and our kids is the Word.

Tragically, too many of us raise children without depositing the Word into their lives. So when tough times arise, and right from wrong decisions need to be made, our kids lack the godly wisdom to know what to do.

Often in therapy I talk with Christian parents who are working through life crises without a knowledge of God's Word. What results is confusion and anxiety; they have no idea how to apply the Scriptures to their problems. Yet if we parents don't have the Word in our hearts, then we are ill-equipped to teach our children. It's not enough for us to depend on a Sunday school teacher to do our job. As parents, it is our responsibility to train up our children in the ways of the Lord.

In the Aftermath, How Shall We Respond?

In every event there are three factors: what happens, the consequences and our response. Spiritually, our first energy must be focused on our responses. You've just read a lot about the events, the behaviors and their consequences—the way all this plays out in life. But what I feel is most important is the state of our souls. What must we do spiritually? What is the greatest challenge?

We must forgive!

The Bible is our guide for this. I personally use the *The Woman's Study Bible*. As I prayed and meditated on these tragic shooting events, I discovered a wonderful teaching on forgiveness that perfectly fits with what I want to share with you.

Steps to Forgiveness[1]

Love is the prime ingredient in forgiveness.

Hatred stirs up quarrels, but love covers all offenses.

—PROVERBS 10:12

Often the one wounded must first forgive *with an act of the will,* allowing time subsequently for the working through of feelings and the experience of healing. Forgiveness comes when we:

1. Remove past offenses from the mind.

No, dear friends, I am still not all I should be, but I am focusing all my energies on this one thing: Forgetting the past and looking forward to what lies ahead, I strain to reach the end of the race and receive the prize for which God, through Christ Jesus, is calling us up to heaven.

—PHILIPPIANS 3:13–14

2. Meditate upon Scripture.

Many persecute and trouble me, yet I have not swerved from your decrees. I hate these traitors because they care nothing for your word. See how I love your commandments, LORD. Give back my life because of your unfailing love. All your words are true; all your just laws will stand forever.

—PSALM 119:157–160

3. Give our hurts over to God.

This suffering is all part of what God has called you to. Christ, who suffered for you, is your example. Follow in his steps. He never sinned, and he never deceived anyone. He did not retaliate when he was insulted. When he suffered, he did not threaten to get even. He left his case in the hands of God, who always judges fairly.

—1 PETER 2:21–23

4. Pray for the offender(s).

As for me, I will certainly not sin against the LORD by ending my prayers for you. And I will continue to teach you what is good and right!

—1 SAMUEL 12:23

But I say, love your enemies! Pray for those who persecute you!

—MATTHEW 5:44

5. Serve as willing vessels of God's grace.

Dear friends, never avenge yourselves. Leave that to God. For it is written, "I will take vengeance; I will repay those who deserve it," says the Lord. Instead, do what the Scriptures say: "If your enemies are hungry, feed them. If they are thirsty, give them something to drink, and they will be ashamed of what they have done to you." Don't let evil get the best of you, but conquer evil by doing good.

—ROMANS 12:19–21

Forgiveness begins in the heart of the Christian. First, we must ask God to forgive us. To do so, we ask the Holy Spirit to reveal any unconfessed offenses in our hearts. That is, am I offended with:

- The killers who killed kids?

- Their parents?

- Other parents and friends?

- The schools and community institutions?

- The media, government and culture?

Once we have confessed any offenses, God is faithful and just to forgive us (1 John 1:9). Although the Word of God is clear regarding what behavior and thoughts are sinful, God commands us not to judge or condemn others (Matt. 7:1).

What is the greatest challenge? We must forgive!

We can now begin to see that God will change the hearts of those caught in the snares of evil. We can also work positively and effectively to bring about change in our culture and institutions to remove violence. Not getting mired in past tragedies, we must move forward, following Christ in addressing His agenda for building God's kingdom.

> I don't mean to say that I have already achieved these things or that I have already reached perfection! But I keep working toward that day when I will finally be all that Christ Jesus saved me for and wants me to be. No, dear friends, I am still not all I should be, but I am focusing all my energies on this one thing: Forgetting the past and looking forward to what lies ahead, I strain to reach the end of the race and receive the prize for which God, through Christ Jesus, is calling us up to heaven.
>
> —PHILIPPIANS 3:12–14

Bible Promises
for Hope and Comfort

*The Bible is a window in this prison of hope,
through which we look into eternity.*

—John Sullivan Dwight

It's easy to succumb to worry and fear when facing the themes we've been discussing in this book. In fact, most of us would agree that life in general is a constant trial, especially if we're parenting teenagers! So where do you go for support, guidance and nurture? Here are some passages of Scripture from the King James Version of the Bible for you and your children to hide in your hearts.

When Fear Takes Over . . .

Be strong and of a good courage, fear not, nor be afraid of them: for the LORD thy God, he it is that doth go with thee; he will not fail thee, nor forsake thee.

—DEUTERONOMY 31:6

Have not I commanded thee? Be strong and of a good courage; be not afraid, neither be thou dismayed: for the LORD thy God is with thee whithersoever thou goest.

—JOSHUA 1:9

The LORD is my light and my salvation; whom shall I fear? the LORD is the strength of my life; of whom shall I be afraid? When the wicked, even mine enemies and my foes, came upon me to eat up my flesh, they stumbled and fell. Though an host should encamp against me, my heart shall not fear: though war should rise against me, in this will I be confident.

—PSALM 27:1–3

For I have heard the slander of many: fear was on every side: while they took counsel together against me, they devised to take away my life.

—PSALM 31:13

Therefore will not we fear, though the earth be removed, and though the mountains be carried into the midst of the sea.

—PSALM 46:2

For God hath not given us the spirit of fear; but of power, and of love, and of a sound mind.

—2 TIMOTHY 1:7

There is no fear in love; but perfect love casteth out fear: because fear hath torment. He that feareth is not made perfect in love.

—1 JOHN 4:18

When You're So Worried . . .

Be careful for nothing; but in every thing by prayer and supplication with thanksgiving let your requests be made known unto God.

And the peace of God, which passeth all understanding, shall keep your hearts and minds through Christ Jesus. . . . Not that I speak in respect of want: for I have learned, in whatsoever state I am, therewith to be content. I know both how to be abased, and I know how to abound: every where and in all things I am instructed both to be full and to be hungry, both to abound and to suffer need. I can do all things through Christ which strengtheneth me.

—PHILIPPIANS 4:6–7, 11–13

But godliness with contentment is great gain. For we brought nothing into this world, and it is certain we can carry nothing out. And having food and raiment let us be therewith content. But they that will be rich fall into temptation and a snare, and into many foolish and hurtful lusts, which drown men in destruction and perdition. For the love of money is the root of all evil: which while some coveted after, they have erred from the faith, and pierced themselves through with many sorrows.

—1 TIMOTHY 6:6–10

When You Feel Depressed . . .

Have mercy upon me, O LORD; for I am weak: O LORD, heal me; for my bones are vexed. My soul is also sore vexed: but thou, O LORD, how long?

—PSALM 6:2–3

And he said unto me, My grace is sufficient for thee: for my strength is made perfect in weakness. Most gladly therefore will I rather glory in my infirmities, that the power of Christ may rest upon me. Therefore I take pleasure in infirmities, in reproaches, in necessities, in persecutions, in distresses for Christ's sake: for when I am weak, then am I strong.

—2 CORINTHIANS 12:9–10

When You Need Wisdom and Guidance in Parenting . . .

Man's goings are of the LORD; how can a man then understand his own way?

—PROVERBS 20:24

Thy word is a lamp unto my feet, and a light unto my path.

—PSALM 119:105

I am thy servant; give me understanding, that I may know thy testimonies.

—PSALM 119:125

If any of you lack wisdom, let him ask of God, that giveth to all men liberally, and upbraideth not; and it shall be given him. But let him ask in faith, nothing wavering. For he that wavereth is like a wave of the sea driven with the wind and tossed. For let not that man think that he shall receive any thing of the Lord. A double minded man is unstable in all his ways.

—JAMES 1:5–8

The fear of the LORD is the beginning of wisdom: a good understanding have all they that do his commandments: his praise endureth for ever.

—PSALM 111:10

For I will give you a mouth and wisdom, which all your adversaries shall not be able to gainsay nor resist.

—LUKE 21:15

Consider what I say; and the Lord give thee understanding in all things.

—2 TIMOTHY 2:7

And we know that the Son of God is come, and hath given us an understanding, that we may know him that is true, and we are in him that is true, even in his Son Jesus Christ. This is the true God, and eternal life.

—1 JOHN 5:20

When Adversity Strikes . . .

Many are the afflictions of the righteous: but the LORD delivereth him out of them all.

—PSALM 34:19

We are troubled on every side, yet not distressed; we are perplexed, but not in despair; Persecuted, but not forsaken; cast down, but not destroyed

—2 CORINTHIANS 4:8–9

My brethren, count it all joy when ye fall into divers temptations; knowing this, that the trying of your faith worketh patience. But let patience have her perfect work, that ye may be perfect and entire, wanting nothing.

—JAMES 1:2–4

So that we ourselves glory in you in the churches of God for your patience and faith in all your persecutions and tribulations that ye endure: Which is a manifest token of the righteous judgment of God, that ye may be counted worthy of the kingdom of God, for which ye also suffer.

—2 THESSALONIANS 1:4–5

Thou therefore endure hardness, as a good soldier of Jesus Christ. No man that warreth entangleth himself with the affairs of this life; that he may please him who hath chosen him to be a soldier. And if a man also strive for masteries, yet is he not crowned, except he strive lawfully.

—2 TIMOTHY 2:3–5

And we know that all things work together for good to them that love God, to them who are the called according to his purpose.

—ROMANS 8:28

When Sadness and Grief Fill Your Days . . .

Therefore the redeemed of the LORD shall return, and come with singing unto Zion; and everlasting joy shall be upon their head: they shall obtain gladness and joy; and sorrow and mourning shall flee away.

—ISAIAH 51:11

Blessed are they that mourn: for they shall be comforted.

—MATTHEW 5:4

Come unto me, all ye that labour and are heavy laden, and I will give you rest. Take my yoke upon you, and learn of me; for I am meek and lowly in heart: and ye shall find rest unto your souls. For my yoke is easy, and my burden is light.

—MATTHEW 11:28–30

Let not your heart be troubled: ye believe in God, believe also in me. In my Father's house are many mansions: if it were not so, I would have told you. I go to prepare a place for you. And if I go and prepare a place for you, I will come again, and receive you unto myself; that where I am, there ye may be also. And whither I go ye know, and the way ye know. Thomas saith unto him, LORD, we know not whither thou goest; and how can we know the way? Jesus saith unto him, I am the way, the truth, and the life: no man cometh unto the Father, but by me.

—JOHN 14:1–6

For though he was crucified through weakness, yet he liveth by the power of God. For we also are weak in him, but we shall live with him by the power of God toward you.

—2 CORINTHIANS 13:4

Now our LORD Jesus Christ himself, and God, even our Father, which hath loved us, and hath given us everlasting consolation and good hope through grace, comfort your hearts, and stablish you in every good word and work.

—2 THESSALONIANS 2:16–17

When You Seek the Sufficiency of Christ ...

My help cometh from the LORD, which made heaven and earth. He will not suffer thy foot to be moved: he that keepeth thee will not slumber.

—PSALM 121.2–3

The LORD is my shepherd; I shall not want. He maketh me to lie down in green pastures: he leadeth me beside the still waters. He restoreth my soul: he leadeth me in the paths of righteousness for his name's sake. Yea, though I walk through the valley of the shadow of death, I will fear no evil: for thou art with me; thy rod and thy staff they comfort me.

—PSALM 23:1–4

And such trust have we through Christ to God-ward: Not that we are sufficient of ourselves to think any thing as of ourselves; but our sufficiency is of God.

—2 CORINTHIANS 3:4–5

I can do all things through Christ which strengtheneth me.

—PHILIPPIANS 4:13

Seeing then that we have a great high priest, that is passed into the heavens, Jesus the Son of God, let us hold fast our profession. For we have not an high priest which cannot be touched with the feeling of our infirmities; but was in all points tempted like as we are, yet without sin. Let us therefore come boldly unto the throne of grace, that we may obtain mercy, and find grace to help in time of need.

—HEBREWS 4:14–16

And when I saw him, I fell at his feet as dead. And he laid his right hand upon me, saying unto me, Fear not; I am the first and the last: I am he that liveth, and was dead; and, behold, I am alive for evermore, Amen; and have the keys of hell and of death.

—REVELATION 1:17–18

When You Long for Peace . . .

And he will destroy in this mountain the face of the covering cast over all people, and the veil that is spread over all nations. He will swallow up death in victory; and the Lord GOD will wipe away tears from off all faces; and the rebuke of his people shall he take away from off all the earth: for the LORD hath spoken it.

—ISAIAH 25:7–8

My covenant was with him of life and peace; and I gave them to him for the fear wherewith he feared me, and was afraid before my name.

—MALACHI 2:5

For he is our peace, who hath made both one, and hath broken down the middle wall of partition between us; having abolished in his flesh the enmity, even the law of commandments contained in ordinances; for to make in himself of twain one new man, so making peace; And that he might reconcile both unto God in one body by the cross, having slain the enmity thereby: And came and preached peace to you which were afar off, and to them that were nigh.

—EPHESIANS 2:14–17

And the peace of God, which passeth all understanding, shall keep your hearts and minds through Christ Jesus. Finally, brethren, whatsoever things are true, whatsoever things are honest, whatsoever things are just, whatsoever things are pure, whatsoever things are lovely, whatsoever things are of good report; if there be any virtue, and if there be any praise, think on these things. Those things, which ye have both learned, and received, and heard, and seen in me, do: and the God of peace shall be with you.

—PHILIPPIANS 4:7–9

When You're Filled With Doubt . . .

God is not a man, that he should lie; neither the son of man, that he should repent. hath he said, and shall he not do it? or hath he spoken, and shall he not make it good?

—NUMBERS 23:19

Trust in the LORD with all thine heart; and lean not unto thine own understanding. In all thy ways acknowledge him, and he shall direct thy paths.

—PROVERBS 3:5–6

For what if some did not believe? shall their unbelief make the faith of God without effect? God forbid: yea, let God be true, but every man a liar.

—ROMANS 3:3–4

Saying, Surely blessing I will bless thee, and multiplying I will multiply thee. And so, after he had patiently endured, he obtained the promise. For men verily swear by the greater: and an oath for confirmation is to them an end of all strife. Wherein God, willing more abundantly to show unto the heirs of promise the immutability of his counsel, confirmed it by an oath: That by two immutable things, in which it was impossible for God to lie, we might have a strong consolation, who have fled for refuge to lay hold upon the hope set before us: Which hope we have as an anchor of the soul, both sure and stedfast, and which entereth into that within the veil.

—HEBREWS 6:14–19

Although the fig tree shall not blossom, neither shall fruit be in the vines; the labour of the olive shall fail, and the fields shall yield no meat; the flock shall be cut off from the fold, and there shall be no herd in the stalls. Yet I will rejoice in the LORD, I will joy in the God of my salvation. The LORD God is my strength, and he will make my feet like hinds' feet, and he will make me to walk upon mine high places.

—HABAKKUK 3:17–19

Then saith he to Thomas, Reach hither thy finger, and behold my hands; and reach hither thy hand, and thrust it into my side: and be not faithless, but believing. And Thomas answered and said unto him, My Lord and my God. Jesus saith unto him, Thomas, because thou hast seen me, thou hast believed: blessed are they that have not seen, and yet have believed. And many other signs truly did Jesus in the presence of his disciples, which are not written in this book. But these are written, that ye might believe that Jesus is the Christ, the Son of God; and that believing ye might have life through his name.

—JOHN 20:27–31

Bring Everything to God in Prayer

Pray without ceasing.

—1 THESSALONIANS 5:17

Be careful for nothing; but in every thing by prayer and supplication with thanksgiving let your requests be made known unto God.

—PHILIPPIANS 4:6

Let us therefore come boldly unto the throne of grace, that we may obtain mercy, and find grace to help in time of need.

—HEBREWS 4:16

Yet have thou respect unto the prayer of thy servant, and to his supplication, O LORD my God, to hearken unto the cry and to the prayer, which thy servant prayeth before thee to day: That thine eyes may be open toward this house night and day, even toward the place of which thou hast said, My name shall be there: that thou mayest hearken unto the prayer which thy servant shall make toward this place. And hearken thou to the supplication of thy servant, and of thy people Israel, when they shall pray toward this place: and hear thou in heaven thy dwelling place: and when thou hearest, forgive.

—1 KINGS 8:28–30

Verily I say unto you, Whatsoever ye shall bind on earth shall be bound in heaven: and whatsoever ye shall loose on earth shall be loosed in heaven.

—MATTHEW 18:18

For we are saved by hope: but hope that is seen is not hope: for what a man seeth, why doth he yet hope for? But if we hope for that we see not, then do we with patience wait for it. Likewise the Spirit also helpeth our infirmities: for we know not what we should pray for as we ought: but the Spirit itself maketh intercession for us with groanings which cannot be uttered. And he that searcheth the hearts knoweth what is the mind of the Spirit, because he maketh intercession for the saints according to the will of God.

—ROMANS 8:24–27

Let us draw near with a true heart in full assurance of faith, having our hearts sprinkled from an evil conscience, and our bodies washed with pure water.

—HEBREWS 10:22

Remember How Much God Loves You!

God created man in his own image, in the image of God created he him; male and female created he them.

—GENESIS 1:27

For we are his workmanship, created in Christ Jesus unto good works, which God hath before ordained that we should walk in them.

—EPHESIANS 2:10

I will praise thee; for I am fearfully and wonderfully made: marvellous are thy works; and that my soul knoweth right well. My substance was not hid from thee, when I was made in secret, and curiously wrought in the lowest parts of the earth. Thine eyes did see my substance, yet being unperfect; and in thy book all my members were written, which in continuance were fashioned, when as yet there was none of them.

—PSALM 139:14–16

O LORD our Lord, how excellent is thy name in all the earth! who hast set thy glory above the heavens. Out of the mouth of babes and sucklings hast thou ordained strength because of thine enemies, that thou mightest still the enemy and the avenger. When I consider thy heavens, the work of thy fingers, the moon and the stars, which thou hast ordained; what is man, that thou art mindful of him? and the son of man, that thou visitest him? For thou hast made him a little lower than the angels, and hast crowned him with glory and honour. Thou madest him to have dominion over the works of thy hands; thou hast put all things under his feet: All sheep and oxen, yea, and the beasts of the field; the fowl of the air, and the fish of the sea, and whatsoever passeth through the paths of the seas. O LORD our Lord, how excellent is thy name in all the earth!

—PSALM 8:1–9

Look Forward to Joy in Heaven

But now is Christ risen from the dead, and become the first-fruits of them that slept. For since by man came death, by man came also the resurrection of the dead. For as in Adam all die, even so in Christ shall all be made alive. But every man in his own order: Christ the firstfruits; afterward they that are Christ's at his coming.

Then cometh the end, when he shall have delivered up the kingdom to God, even the Father; when he shall have put down all rule and all authority and power. For he must reign, till he hath put all enemies under his feet. The last enemy that shall be destroyed is death. For he hath put all things under his feet. But when he saith all things are put under him, it is manifest that he is excepted, which did put all things under him. And when all things shall be subdued unto him, then shall the Son also himself be subject unto him that put all things under him, that God may be all in all.

—1 Corinthians 15:20–28

Now this I say, brethren, that flesh and blood cannot inherit the kingdom of God; neither doth corruption inherit incorruption. Behold, I shew you a mystery; we shall not all sleep, but we shall all be changed, in a moment, in the twinkling of an eye, at the last trump: for the trumpet shall sound, and the dead shall be raised incorruptible, and we shall be changed. For this corruptible must put on incorruption, and this mortal must put on immortality. So when this corruptible shall have put on incorruption, and this mortal shall have put on immortality, then shall be brought to pass the saying that is written, Death is swallowed up in victory. O death, where is thy sting? O grave, where is thy victory? The sting of death is sin; and the strength of sin is the law. But thanks be to God, which giveth us the victory through our Lord Jesus Christ. Therefore, my beloved brethren, be ye stedfast, unmoveable, always abounding in the work of the Lord, foras-much as ye know that your labour is not in vain in the Lord.

—1 CORINTHIANS 15:50–58

But I would not have you to be ignorant, brethren, con-cerning them which are asleep, that ye sorrow not, even as others which have no hope. For if we believe that Jesus died and rose again, even so them also which sleep in Jesus will God bring with him.

—1 THESSALONIANS 4:13–14

For we know that if our earthly house of this tabernacle were dissolved, we have a building of God, an house not made with hands, eternal in the heavens. For in this we groan, earnestly desiring to be clothed upon with our house which is from heaven: If so be that being clothed we shall not be found naked. For we that are in this tabernacle do groan, being bur-dened: not for that we would be unclothed, but clothed upon, that mortality might be swallowed up of life. Now he that hath wrought us for the selfsame thing is God, who also hath given unto us the earnest of the Spirit. Therefore we are always confident, knowing that, whilst we are at home in the body, we are absent from the Lord: (For we walk by faith, not by sight:) We are confident, I say, and willing rather to be absent from the body, and to be present with the Lord.

—2 CORINTHIANS 5:1–8

And I saw a new heaven and a new earth: for the first heaven and the first earth were passed away; and there was no more sea. And I John saw the holy city, new Jerusalem, coming down from God out of heaven, prepared as a bride adorned for her husband. And I heard a great voice out of heaven saying, Behold, the tabernacle of God is with men, and he will dwell with them, and they shall be his people, and God himself shall be with them, and be their God. And God shall wipe away all tears from their eyes; and there shall be no more death, neither sorrow, nor crying, neither shall there be any more pain: for the former things are passed away.

—REVELATION 21:1–4

For our conversation is in heaven; from whence also we look for the Saviour, the Lord Jesus Christ: Who shall change our vile body, that it may be fashioned like unto his glorious body, according to the working whereby he is able even to subdue all things unto himself. Therefore, my brethren dearly beloved and longed for, my joy and crown, so stand fast in the Lord, my dearly Beloved.

—PHILIPPIANS 3:20–4:1

May the name of Jesus, the Son of God, who is mightier than all the hosts of Satan, and more glorious than all the angels of heaven, abide with you in your going out and your coming in; by day and by night; at morning and evening; at all times and in all places.

May the name of Jesus protect and deliver you from the wrath of evil persons; from the assaults of evil spirits; from foes invisible; from the snares of the Evil One; and from all low passions that beguile the soul and the body.

May the name of Jesus protect and deliver you. And the blessing of God Almighty, Father, Son and Holy Spirit, be with you this day and always.

AMEN[1]

Generational Curses

In the process of viewing these high-school shoot-ings from a spiritual perspective, some rough ques-tions arise concerning two issues: Generational curses and Satanic influences. While this book cannot be a comprehensive guide for these issues, we do want to address these concerns briefly as they relate to these tragedies.

> Thou shalt not bow down thyself to them, nor serve them: for I the LORD thy God am a jealous God, visiting the iniquity of the fathers upon the children unto the third and fourth generation of them that hate me; and shewing mercy unto thousands of them that love me, and keep my commandments
>
> —EXODUS 20:5–6, KJV

Our children and children's children are vulnerable to attack when our sins are passed on to them. We observe examples of generational curses throughout our society—abusers often are children or grandchildren of abusers; addicts are often the children or grandchildren of addicts; evil parents beget evil children and grand-children. So the sins of our culture's parents and grand-parents does become a curse for today's generation.

We do not have to recite the litany of rebellion and abuse that arose in the sixties and seventies to make the case for problems at the turn of the millennium. Our generation is littered with the garbage passed on to us from our predecessors. The question is not, "Do we suffer under a sin curse from prior generations?" For the answer to the question abounds not only in societal evil surrounding us but also in Scripture, which reveals:

> Against thee, thee only, have I sinned, and done this evil in thy sight: that thou mightest be justi-fied when thou speakest, and be clear when thou judgest. Behold, I was shapen in iniquity, and in sin did my mother conceive me.Behold, thou desirest truth in the inward parts: and in the hidden part thou shalt make me to know wisdom.
> —PSALM 51:4–6, KJV

At the root of the curse lies original sin. And the axe to cut off the root is the cross of Christ. Our spiritual response today must be the same as in the first century A.D. The Bible clearly reveals what breaks the curse. The apostle Paul writes,

> But that no man is justified by the law in the sight of God, it is evident: for, The just shall live by faith. And the law is not of faith: but, The man that doeth them shall live in them. Christ hath redeemed us from the curse of the law, being

made a curse for us: for it is written, Cursed is
every one that hangeth on a tree: That the
blessing of Abraham might come on the Gentiles
through Jesus Christ; that we might receive the
promise of the Spirit through faith.

—GALATIANS 3:11–14

What breaks generational curses is the shed blood of
Christ. When we are saved, the curse is broken. Past sin
has no power over us. We walk in the Spirit and not
according to the flesh. Paul writes,

There is therefore now no condemnation to them
which are in Christ Jesus, who walk not after the
flesh, but after the Spirit. For the law of the Spirit
of life in Christ Jesus hath made me free from the
law of sin and death.

—ROMANS 8:1–2, KJV

Those who are carnally minded find themselves controlled by the world and its influences—music, video
games, violence, addictions, bondages and curses. But
those who have been set free by Christ Jesus have the
power both to resist the world's violent ways and also to
pass on to their children and children's children the
blessings of knowing Jesus.

Demonic, Satanic and Evil Influences

Satan's dark powers certainly control those under his
dominion. About such people Paul writes,

Put on the whole armour of God, that ye may be
able to stand against the wiles of the devil. For we

> wrestle not against flesh and blood, but against
> principalities, against powers, against the rulers of
> the darkness of this world, against spiritual
> wickedness in high places. Wherefore take unto
> you the whole armour of God, that ye may be able
> to withstand in the evil day, and having done all,
> to stand.
> —EPHESIANS 6:11–13, KJV

Just as Satan manipulated and controlled Judas (Luke 22:3, 31; John 13:26), he seeks to use evil and wicked people to attack believers. We are to love the lost and share with them the gospel of Christ. But we are also to resist the ways of wickedness and the temptations used by those controlled by the rulers of darkness and spiritual wickedness in high places.

Believers who allow themselves and their families to be exposed to the evil will find themselves under demonic attack. To protect against such attacks, believing parents and children must:

- Avoid watching or listening to violence through any form of media—TV, Internet, movies, music or games.

- Take a stand in our culture against evil and wickedness especially as it is manifested in public media and institutions.

- Pray and stand firm in God's Word knowing the devices of Satan (2 Cor. 2:11).

- Work with the school systems to keep violence—a device of Satan—out of the schools.

- Continue to advocate for prayer and free expressions of Christian faith in the public schools.

We believe that the removal of prayer from the schools in the sixties correlates directly with the increase of violence, evil and Satanic influences in our schools.

Notes

Preface

1. From *Moving Target*, a video series by Nicky Cruz, 1999.

Chapter 1

It Couldn't Happen Here

1. *Chicago Sun-Times*, April 28, 1999, 49.
2. Jonathan Alter, "On the Cusp of a Crusade," *Newsweek*, May 10, 1999.
3. Lynn Bartels, "Parents' Worst Nightmare: 'It's Dylan,'" www.InsideDenver.com, April 29, 1999.
4. Jerry Adler and Karen Springen, "How to Fight Back," *Newsweek*, May 3, 1999, 37.
5. John Hendren, "Internet Provides Bomb Blueprints," www.ap.org, April 26, 1999.
6. From Parents Resource Institute for Drug Education.
7. This list of statistics comes from *Code Blue* (Ann Arbor, MI: Servant Publications, 1995), 26, and The National Center for Education, as quoted on www.ap.org, April 28, 1999.
8. *Code Blue*, 27.

Chapter 2

Lost Boys and Private Pain

1. Matt Bai, "Anatomy of a Massacre," *Newsweek*, May 3, 1999, 26.
2. These adolescent stages are adapted and summarized from the American Academy of Child and Adolescent Psychology at Indiana University.
3. Cliff Schimmels, *What Parents Try to Forget About Adolescence* (Elgin, IL: LifeJourney Books, 1989), quote on the half-title page.
4. This description of depression is adapted from guidelines in the *Diagnostic and Statistical Manual, Vol. IV.*
5. Quote from Dave Veerman, source unknown.
6. John Cloud, "What Can the Schools Do?" *Time*, May 3, 1999, 39.
7. Anna Mulrine, "Once bullied, now bullies—with guns," *U.S. News & World Report*, May 3, 1999, 24.
8. John Cloud, "What Can the Schools Do?" *Time*, May 3, 1999, 38.
9. S. I. Hayakawa, cited in Lloyd Cory, ed., *Quote, Unquote* (Wheaton, IL: Scripture Press, 1977).

Chapter 3

Relational Pain: From the Roots Up

1. Amy Dickinson, "Where Were the Parents?" *Time*, May 3, 1999, 40.
2. Barbara Bush as quoted in *Women's Wisdom Through the Ages* (Wheaton, IL: Harold Shaw Publishers), 85.
3. Edith Shaeffer, "What Is a Family?", quoted in *Women's Wisdom Through the Ages*, 83.
4. Carole Sanderson Streeter, "Finding Your Place After Divorce," quoted in *Women's Wisdom Through the Ages*, 94.

5. Amy Dickinson, "Where Were the Parents?" *Time*, May 3, 1999, 40.

6. Preston Gillham, "Lifetime Guarantee," a quote in Stu Webber, *Tender Warrior* (Sisters, OR: Questar Publishers, 1993).

7. Patrick Morley, *Walking With Christ in the Details of Life* (Nashville: Thomas Nelson), as quoted in *New Man*, March/April 1995.

8. Adam Cohen, "A Curse of Cliques," *Time*, May 3, 1999, 45.

9. Nancy Gibbs, "The Littleton Massacre," *Time*, May 3, 1999, 31.

10. Ron Luce, *Inspire the Fire* (Lake Mary, FL: Creation House Publishers, 1994), quoted by Gary Wilde in *Mentoring* (Colorado Springs: Chariot Victor Books, 1997), 27.

Chapter 4

Cultural Pain: Media Influences

1. John Leo, "When life imitates video," *U.S. News & World Report*, May 3, 1999, 14.

2. Ted Turner quote, *Los Angeles Times*, March 3, 1999.

3. National Coalition on TV Violence, "Violence in Cartoons Increases," *NCTV News*, June-August 1991, 7.

4. Milton Chen, Ph.D., *The Smart Parent's Guide to Kid's TV* (San Francisco: KQED Books, 1994), 83.

5. Leonard Eron quote on TV violence, as quoted by Wendy L. Josephson, Ph.D., for the Department of Canadian Heritage, February 1995. Reprinted by the Media Awareness Network with permission of the Minister of Public Works and Government Services, Canada.

6. Adapted from Wendy L. Josephson, Ph.D., *op. cit.*

7. The National Television Violence Study, 1994–95.

8. Dr. Carol S. Kennedy in an article for the *Oviedo Voice*, April 29, 1999.

9. "Voices of a Generation," *Newsweek*, May 10, 1999, 46.

10. Wilson and Hunter, 1983.

11. Wendy L. Josephson, *op. cit.*

12. This guideline uses ideas adapted from *The Media-Wise Family* by Ted Baehr (Colorado Springs: ChariotVictor Publishing, 1998).

13. Dave Allocca, "Bereaved Families Point Finger at Leo's Diaries," ABC News Internet Ventures, April 12, 1999.

14. "Testimony of the American Academy of Pediatrics on the Social Impact of Music Violence" before the Senate Subcommittee on Oversight of Government Management, Restructuring and the District of Columbia presented by Frank Palumbo, M.D., November 6, 1997.

15. "The Music/Violence Connection," Musician's Exchange Web site, April 25, 1999.

16. "Senate Panel Tunes Into Music Violence," Reuters, November 8, 1997.

17. Funk and Buchman, "Playing Violent Video and Computer Games and Adolescent Self-Concept," *Journal of Communication*, 1996.

18. John Leland, "The Secret Life of Teens," *Newsweek*, May 10, 1999, 48.

19. John Leo, "When life imitates video," *U.S. News & World Report*, May 3, 1999, 14.

20. Sissela Bok, *Mayhem: Violence As Public Entertainment* (Reading, MA: Addison/Wesley, 1998).

21. Public policy statement, Mothers Against Violence in America.

22. Gerald Levin in a speech given to the Hollywood Radio and Television Society at Regent Beverly Wilshire Hotel.

23. John Leland, "The Secret Life of Teens," *Newsweek*, May 10, 1999, 4647.

Chapter 5

Emotional Pain: Dealing With Death

1. S. G. Weizman and P. Kamm, *About Mourning, Support and Guidance for the Bereaved* (New York: Human Sciences Press, 1984).
2. Dustin Scholle as quoted in *Chicago Tribune*, May 2, 1999.
3. Associated Press, U.S., April 25, 1999.
4. Ibid.
5. Acute Stress Disorder list of symptoms adapted from DSM-IV, published by the American Psychiatric Association, 1994.
6. Post-Traumatic Stress Disorder list of symptoms adapted from DSM-IV, published by the American Psychiatric Association, 1994.
7. Delores Kuenning, *Helping People Through Grief* (Minneapolis, MN: Bethany House Publishers, 1987), 193f.
8. *Chicago Tribune*, May 2, 1999, 2.
9. *Chicago Tribune*, May 2, 1999, 8.

Chapter 6

A Faith Perspective on School Violence

1. Dr. Martin Luther King, Jr., as quoted on a record album sleeve of *U2 Pride (In the Name of Love)* by U2.
2. Chuck Colson, Breakpoint Commentary, April 26, 1997.
3. *USA Today*, March 3, 1999, 7A.
4. Ibid.
5. R. G. Lee.

Postscript

The Aftermath: The Most Important Thing Left to Do

1. Adapted from *The Woman's Study Bible* (Nashville: Thomas Nelson Publishers, 1995), 1730.

Appendix

Bible Promises for Hope and Comfort

1. Adapted from *Christarakana: The Book of Common Prayer of India, Pakistan, Burma and Ceylon.*

You can experience more of *God's grace & love!*

If you would like free information on how you can know God more deeply and experience His grace, love and power more fully in your life, simply write or e-mail us. We'll be delighted to send you information that will be a blessing to you.

To check out other titles from **Creation House** that will impact your life, be sure to visit your local Christian bookstore, or call this toll-free number to learn the location of the Christian retailer nearest you: **1-800-991-7747**

For free information from Creation House:

CREATION HOUSE
600 Rinehart Rd.
Lake Mary, FL 32746
www.creationhouse.com